HAVE YOU JUST ABOUT GIVEN UP LOOKING FOR MR. RIGHT?

1. Does it seem that all the "good men" are taken? ❑ yes ❑ no

2. Are you frustrated going to bars, dances, and health clubs hoping to connect with Mr. Right? ❑ yes ❑ no

3. Are you about to settle for Mr. HoHum because you cannot find Mr. Right in your town? ❑ yes ❑ no

4. Are you continually disappointed with men because they just don't measure up to your Dad? ❑ yes ❑ no

5. Are you still going to the same places doing the same things with the same people and never meeting the man you are looking for? ❑ yes ❑ no

6. Are you waiting for God to mysteriously deliver your future husband to you without you having to do anything? ❑ yes ❑ no

7. Do you think living with someone is a practical way to prepare for a strong marriage? ❑ yes ❑ no

8. Do you think that once you are married your real life will finally begin? ❑ yes ❑ no

9. Do you find yourself believing that he is "the one" every time you start to date someone? ❑ yes ❑ no

10. Do you find yourself in abusive relationships but always believe this one will be different? ❑ yes ❑ no

If you've answered any of these questions "Yes," then I urge you to read *Finding Mr. Right,* and begin taking steps toward the relationship you've always hoped for.

FINDING
MR. RIGHT

FINDING MR. RIGHT

[AND HOW TO KNOW WHEN YOU HAVE]

STEPHEN ARTERBURN
AND
Dr. MEG J. RINCK

THOMAS NELSON
Since 1798

NASHVILLE   DALLAS   MEXICO CITY   RIO DE JANEIRO

Published in Nashville, Tennessee, by Thomas Nelson. Thomas Nelson is a registered trademark of Thomas Nelson, Inc.

Thomas Nelson, Inc., titles may be purchased in bulk for educational, business, fund-raising, or sales promotional use. For information, please e-mail SpecialMarkets@ThomasNelson.com.

ISBN 978-0-7852-7802-3 (HC)
ISBN 978-0-7852-6277-0 (TP)
Library of Congress Control Number: 2001 135271

Printed in the United States of America.

10 11 12 13 WC 15 14 13 12

For all the women who hold us men to a higher standard,
this one's for you.

—STEVE ARTERBURN

To my mom, Bee Forbes Josephson,
who sure knew Mr. RIGHT when she saw him over 55 years ago!
Way to go, Mom!

—Love and thanks, MEG :-)
your eldest child, and first daughter

CONTENTS

CONTENTS

PART III: THE SEARCH

PART IV: WHEN THE SEARCH IS OVER

PREFACE

Last year we published *Avoiding Mr. Wrong (And What to Do if You Didn't): The Ten Men Who Will Ruin Your Life.* The book was a great success and even won awards. The publisher has now made it available in paperback. Salon Magazine selected it as one of the top ten publications of 2000. As of this writing it is a nominee for the Gold Medallion Award, an honor presented for writing excellence by the Evangelical Christian Publishing Association. That it was nominated from thousands of other books earned it a Silver Medallion.

These and other honors are very gratifying, but not nearly as much as the letters and e-mails we received indicating that the book had helped women identify and avoid the wrong kind of guy. We loved the letters from parents who bought copies for their teenage daughters. One young woman bought the book, confronted her sister the week before her wedding, convinced her she was marrying the wrong man, and they called off the wedding. The sister courageously realized it was far better returning wedding gifts than having them thrown at her.

Unfortunately, the most common comment we heard was a question: "Where was this book thirty years ago when I needed it?" It is sad that so many listened to the most common advice about picking a mate: "You'll just know."

The response to the book about the wrong guys motivated us to write this companion about the right guys. In gardening terms, we did not just want to write about weeds, we wanted to present the beauty of roses too.

It is our desire that this book be informative, entertaining, and practical. It is also our desire that when you finish it you will pass it along to someone else who could use it. Our dream is that every teenage girl reads it so she will have a better understanding of who the good guys are and how to spot them. Thank you for taking the time to read this. We hope the answers you seek are within these covers.

STEPHEN ARTERBURN
MEG JOSEPHSON RINCK

INTRODUCTION

Here is a question for you as you start off with us on the journey to finding Mr. Right: Should you be looking for Mr. Right?

Some find the idea pretty demeaning to both men and women. After all, shopping for a new coat is one thing; hunting for a man is something else. Isn't it?

Some women are really put off by the idea of "looking" for someone at all. They do not see themselves as "desperate and dateless," or at least not desperate, and do not want to spend their weekends in some singles "meat market" environment.

Then again, today, many women feel perfectly happy flying solo. No longer economically dependent on men, and able to have a full sexual life without fear of pregnancy, many ask, "Who needs them?" No longer do they postpone the adult trappings of a home, car, travel, or children until the right man comes along. Twenty percent of all homes sold in 1999 were sold to single women.[1] *Time*/CNN found in a year 2000 poll that 61 percent of women ages eighteen to forty-nine would now consider raising a child on their own by choice. This more independent, gutsy, happy-being-alone woman has become the millennium's heroine. One has only to note the popularity of such television shows as *Sex in the City* or *Judging Amy* to realize there has been a cultural shift.

No longer are unmarried women over thirty years old considered "spinsters" or social outcasts. Young women nowadays don't fear being old maids as much as they worry about "not being themselves." Self-actualization, self-worth, and self-fulfillment may take precedent over early commitment to a long-term relationship. Many are willing to risk commitment to adopted children or those created via sperm donors, but they would never put themselves into the hands of "a controlling man" by marrying him. So, to these women, the idea of looking for Mr. Right is laughable.

Other women have been out there in the "meat market," and they don't like it any more than the independent women. They just have different reasons for hating it. They are tired of being ogled by guys at dances or singles bars. Weary of chance encounters, they are looking for a permanent relationship. They are willing if not eager to "look" but resist the popular methods of doing so. Often these women are more than thirty years old and are beginning to question if they made the right decision when they chose to postpone marriage until after their careers were established. They have experienced the glamorous (and sometimes not-so-glamorous) single-woman routine, and they are sick of it. What they long for most is the companionship a permanent relationship in marriage would bring.

Loneliness is the shadow that awaits them when they come home from work each night. They long for the comfort of someone to crawl into bed next to (besides the dog). They miss having a shared history with someone over a long period of time. Every couple of months they feel blue and wonder if perhaps they should have settled for that guy right out of college. So they are starting to look for Mr. Right, but they do not think that they will find him anywhere they have been lately.

Some younger women, usually twenty-somethings, are so used to "hooking up" for chance and purely sexual one-night stands that the whole concept of Mr. Right seems funny. All they are looking for is a good time. The idea that anyone would even consider anything else is silly to them. They see themselves as too young for a relationship. They just want to have fun.

For the uninitiated, "hooking up" is the widespread practice on college campuses of young adults going out to a bar or a frat house or a dance, all dressed up and mentally psyched to pick someone to have sex with that night. The rules of hooking up are that you do not expect to see the person again after that evening; and that you get sufficiently intoxicated to "do it" but not so drunk you put yourself in danger. Hooking up is popular for many reasons, not the least of which is that it involves no commitment beyond the moment, which is appealing to students who often take a full load of classes and work besides. It is the modern way of having your cake and eating it, too, since most young people who engage in hooking up have every intention of settling down and marrying "someday," but not until they are educationally and financially settled.

Certain women see looking for Mr. Right as ridiculous for entirely different reasons than the twenty-something women do. They are usually more than forty years old and widowed or divorced. They have already had enough experience with men to conclude (rightfully, in their minds) that there are not any good men out there, and if there are, they are all taken. Usually cynical and bitter from past relationships, these women have given up. They think there is no point looking because there is no one worth finding. At best, men are boors, dogs, ingrates, or babies.

Note the popular bumper sticker: "So many men, so little intelligence." Angry and resentful, these women have had it with men. Perhaps in their heart of hearts they would love to find a good man but honestly do not believe they ever will. Some of you may see their attitude as a bit of sour grapes, but to them it is based on very real hurt from their own disappointing experiences.

Then you run into the holier-than-thou crowd who use the Bible to justify a choice for lifelong singleness. These women take the apostle Paul literally when he wrote to the Corinthians, "It is good for a man not to marry" (1 Cor. 7:1). They are "above" the need or desire for a spouse. Never mind that Paul was talking about first-century life, where people never knew if they would live from one hour to the next, due to the intense persecution of Christians. The Romans were beheading Christians right and left! So it was not exactly the time to run off and get married. But Paul's much bigger point was to instruct singles to go ahead and marry rather than destroy themselves or compromise out of uncontrolled desired or lust. Of course it would be better to be under control, but Paul's practical advice makes good sense and indicates he was not against the institution of marriage.

These twenty-first-century women inappropriately use Scripture to justify a stance that marriage and commitment and sex are for lower spiritual beings who are still tied to the flesh. So they view looking for Mr. Right as a less-than-noble activity.

There are still others in the church crowd who have kissed looking for Mr. Right good-bye. These women believe that God has each life all mapped out and He will bring the right person to their doorstep. If that were the case, most of us would be married to the one who delivers the mail. Whether they are sincere in their belief or using it as a way to avoid rejection, they choose not to involve themselves in a search for the right man.

If you are one of the folks who is not looking or you are avoiding marriage like the plague, we have some shocking news for you. Marriage is actually good for you! Recent research has shown that marriage is the best tonic for mental health. Over a five-year period, getting married or staying married reduces depression more than being single or getting divorced. This may be because of feelings of emotional support, stability, and commitment come from being married. Even unhappily-marrieds do better mentally than those who are single.[2]

If you are single and dating, waiting to date, or through with dating, there are some questions you might be asking, such as: Where do I get guidelines for the right view of sex, love, and marriage? How do I decide if this or that man is right for me? What can I do to attract Mr. Right? Am I supposed to be out looking for the right man? If so, *how* do I find him?

All of these are important questions that we hope this book will help you answer for your own life. Let's look at the biggie first.

SEARCHING FOR MR. RIGHT— AND BEING MS. RIGHT

Is it okay to look for Mr. Right? We think so. But more important—and a major premise of this book—you need to be making yourself right for the moment you find him (if you do). There is no guarantee that if you show enough faith or service or try to do the right thing that God is going to land a good one for you. You may bargain with God and negotiate a lifestyle in exchange for a mate, and God still may not deliver. That is a tough reality, especially for some very faithful believers. But it is true. And it is an encouragement to all who are single not to wait for Mr. Right before you engage in life to the fullest. So we say, "Look!" And while you are looking, "Live!" And as you live, love yourself enough to become the best you can be, future husband or no future husband.

Should looking for Mr. Right be the most important thing in your life? We do not think so. We think that the most important aspect of life is a relationship with God. Your desire or search for Mr. Right should never take precedence over your desire and search for God. That to which we devote ourselves will shape us. If we build our happiness solely around one person, we will be keenly disappointed. Human beings, even good ones, will fail us. We will fail them too. Only God will be faithful in every circumstance.

We must seek God first, trust Him to provide for us and meet our needs even if He does not meet every desire. That relationship with God should be so liberating that you feel free to live with or without a man and still enjoy meaning and fulfillment in your life.

If it is legitimate to look for Mr. Right, how do you go about it? First, begin with being intentional. Do you know what that means? If someone intentionally steps on your foot, he meant to do it. He thought about it, planned it, and did it. Someone once said, "If you aim at nothing, you will be sure to hit it." Many women never find a good life partner because they did not aim at the right target. They do not know how to be intentional.

Let's say you want to get married, have 2.5 kids, live in a nice house, and be able to provide decently, but not necessarily extravagantly, for your children. Would it make sense to drop out of high school, stay home and sponge off Mom and Dad, and sleep with anyone who comes along? Of course not. If you want these positive things you have to take positive actions to achieve them. You graduate from high school, go to college or vocational school, work hard, save your money, and hang around other people who have similar values. You do not waste your money on things that are gone in a day. You spend your time bettering yourself, so that you become a well-rounded, attractive, healthy person.

You start to demonstrate to the world that you are a woman of worth and value. You gear all of your decisions toward your goal of attracting a responsible spouse and eventually becoming a loving parent within the bonds of marriage. You do not listen to people who say it is okay to fool around now because you can settle down later. You realize that today *is* the first day of the rest of your life and that the seemingly small decisions you are making today *will* shape all of your tomorrows.

You do not look to run into Mr. Right in a bar, a dance hall, or a crack house. You expect to find him at church, in school, or at the gym. You deliberately put yourself where you are apt to meet someone who wants to go where you do, not someone who only wants to go to bed. If your town is small and there are few single people there, you investigate cities and towns elsewhere. You look for schools, jobs, opportunities in geographical locations where many other single people live and work.

In the early eighties, for example, Dallas was a city that was booming with jobs and singles. Three of Meg's four sisters moved there within a year of each other, and within a few years all of them had met their husbands through local churches. They could have stayed where the odds of meeting a fine Christian man were fewer, but they decided to be smart and go where they would be likely to find a single man.

The point is be intentional about your goal. Make decisions that support the goal of finding Mr. Right.

Second, make yourself into the kind of woman for whom Mr. Right is looking. For example, if you want to find an interesting conversationalist, then check out your own chatting skills. What interesting conversationalist wants to talk to someone who can say only "Ya know" and "Like, it's like . . ."? If you want a guy who is physically active but you are a couch potato, guess what? You will genuinely need to change yourself if you want to attract someone with those qualities.

These are just a couple of ideas we want to plant in your mind as you read. Yes, you can look for Mr. Right. You can prepare. And we want to help. So let's get going!

PART 1

FIRST
STEPS

CHAPTER 1

ONLY ONE MR. RIGHT?

Avoiding Mr. Wrong is one thing. Finding Mr. Right is another. What does it mean to "find Mr. Right"? Some people wonder if there even is a "Mr. Right" for every woman. Others believe there are any number of "right" partners out there and it is just a matter of choosing one. How do you know who is a Mr. Right, anyway? Is what is right for you, right for your best friend? Some people are sure there are things you can do to maximize your chances of finding Mr. Right. Others question whether being Ms. Right has anything to do with finding Mr. Right. Is there someone who is "God's will" for you more than someone else? How will you know when you find him?

Avoiding Mr. Wrong is one thing, but finding Mr. Right involves much more. Avoiding is the prevention step, but finding leads to connection that can either build a life or break a spirit.

If these are things you are concerned about, you have picked up the right book. We know that many women have learned to spot a Mr. Wrong when they see him coming. Yet they are at a loss in trying to discern what makes a man a good marriage partner. (Note we said *good*, not perfect. No man or woman is a flawless spouse.) You can, however, find a man who is likely to be a lifelong, loving husband rather than a man who is doomed to failure from the get-go. We will show you how. But first, that nagging question:

ONE OR NONE?

Is there only one right person out there? If so, what if you miss him—can you expect only a life of loneliness and misery? Some women believe that fate or God has picked one right mate for them, and they are on a desperate search to find that guy. Woe to the woman who takes the wrong path. She is forever stuck with God's "second best."

In these women's view, as if it is not hard enough to discover the path to the "right" one, God seems to take a sadistic pleasure in being silent or unwilling to give them a clue when they need it. So these women either become so picky that no one will do, or they rely on magical thinking, other people's opinions, or some sort of mystical guidance (such as closing their eyes and letting their Bible fall open to a passage and taking that for God's will). They may be so afraid of making the "wrong" choice that they never make one at all and move from relationship to relationship, unable to commit.

One young couple heard at their church that whomever they felt least attracted to was the one God wanted them to marry. After all, the theory went, our ways are not God's ways. We would be attracted to someone and desire someone who would fulfill our worldly needs but not our spiritual needs. To some that may sound quite extreme. But we have many friends miserably married because they thought that if they were attracted to someone, it must be the wrong person. One couple married, even though they were not at all attracted, nor felt any love for each other. They produced five children, and then the woman fell in love with someone. She left the church and her family and married her lover. Her husband wanted to do the right thing so he retained custody of the kids and refused to remarry. So because of a false teaching from a well-meaning church, a well-meaning man will remain unmarried and raise his kids alone. A well-meaning woman will pursue her dreams, and in the wake of all these mistakes, the children will suffer needlessly. If the children don't get help, they will also feel the impact of erroneous teaching as they grow up and become adults.

Other women seem to take the view that rather than there being only one right person, almost anyone will do. If he is male, living, and able to crawl to the altar, he is marriage material. It is as if these women turn off their brains when it comes to picking marriage partners. They may be bright, well educated, have good jobs. No matter— they still are clueless when it comes to men.

Other women are young, uneducated, and desperately lonely. They are flattered that some guy (any guy) is paying attention to them. Gullible, they believe his profession of "love" and often, since they believe in the concept of love at first sight, they wed quickly and blindly.

Some women cannot be happy with the "right" man. They may have found a guy who, it would seem, was Mr. Right in every way. One man met his wife in Bible school. They dated, fell in love, and because of common goals and mutual dedication to God and ministry, decided to marry. They began their life together pastoring a small church. Everything seemed fine at first. Their training held them in good stead, and they were beginning to see fruit in their work together.

Then, about two years into the marriage, she was the most miserable woman you could imagine. There was nothing he could do right. She picked at everything he did. In her mind he just was not good enough, not close to the man she had always dreamed she would marry. She was miserable, and she made his life miserable also. Finally, she had no interest in him or anything of his ministry. Her expectations run wild just could not be matched.

Her actions broke his heart. He begged her to go to counseling, but she refused. The husband went to counseling alone. He stuck with this woman, hoping she would come to herself and come back to him and God. Finally, she was unfaithful to him, and her promiscuity made clear that her decision was final . Reluctantly, he divorced her. In this case it appears that a woman did not know a good thing—a faithful, devoted husband—when she had it.

Another woman actively pursued a relationship with a shy, kind-hearted fellow at her office. He was quiet but honest, hardworking, and faithful. He did not drink, smoke, or use pornography. While not over-religious, he did believe in God and held to Judeo-Christian values. He had not dated much and was flattered that she was interested in him. Frugal but not tight, he enjoyed buying her little surprises and gifts for special occasions. She was eager to meet his extended family, and her family embraced him warmly as well. They were married in her church.

Almost immediately his family noticed a chill in their relationship. When invited to a family gathering, she always had a reason not to come. So at first, he did not come either. Then he began to come alone. No one could figure it out. He seemed sad, but no one wanted to intrude. After three or four years, she announced that she wanted a divorce. He asked for counseling; he talked to her parents; he talked to his parents. All she would say was that he was boring. After they separated it became common knowledge around their small town that she was having an affair with a bartender in the next village. Before the divorce was even final, she was pregnant and living with this other man.

Some women cannot spot a Mr. Right even when they are married to him!

Certain women despair of the whole thing and become cynical. "There are no good men out there!" they cry. Bitter over past abusive relationships or perhaps because of a cruel father or brother, they doubt any man can be a good person. "All men want is sex." "Men want only to control you." "You cannot trust any of them. They are all liars." "Men do not care about anything but themselves. Give them a beer and a babe, and they are happy." "Men are such babies. They cannot handle anything inconvenient, painful, or difficult. You have to protect them from everything, or they lose it." The women who believe these things end up living angry, lonely, empty lives.

Some women get so turned off by the bad behaviors certain men exhibit that they turn to the lesbian lifestyle as their answer to finding the "right" partner. They feel safer, more understood, and more in control with another woman. They extrapolate their own bad experience with men to all men and make sad choices.

SOME BASIC ASSUMPTIONS

We want to set forth our basic assumptions about this matter of finding the "right" man. In that way you will understand our perspective as we go through the book together.

We believe that there *are* good men out there. While no man is perfect, there are thousands of moral, kind, hardworking, faithful, fun-loving, intelligent, sincere men who are looking for women with similar qualities. Some men used to be Mr. Wrong and learned through hard knocks, and /or a divorce, where they messed up. They have genuinely changed. They have developed new priorities. They have proven themselves consistent, honest, and faithful.

Some have been Mr. Right all their lives but were dumped by a Ms. Wrong and desperately hurt. Some may be shy or quiet, or plain in looks, but they are gems nonetheless. Some are basically Mr. Right but have gotten off-track for a bit. They are diamonds in the rough, and the right prospector knows how to bring out their true quality.

We assume that there are basic qualities that make a person a desirable marriage partner and qualities that make a person a dangerous risk.

No one has all good qualities and no bad ones, but there are certain characteristics that good men have in common. Obviously, Mr. Right is going to have more good qualities than bad.

In our view there is no one right or perfect person for everyone. There may be any number of men who could be Mr. Right for you. Each person who comes along will have good and bad qualities. Sure, someone else may come along in a year or two who would be better in this area or that, but that does not mean the man you chose was the "wrong" one.

Based on this, you want to date the men that have the greatest chance of being your Mr. Right based on their character and common interests. You want to do whatever you can to find a man that has the most of what you have been looking for in a man. But once you marry and commit, you have just discovered Mr. Right. He may not be as right as someone else could have been, but because you picked him, God takes him and makes him your Mr. Right. You will have problems, some more than others, but you cannot use the excuse that he was not the right one to justify moving on to someone else. You could potentially commit to any number of people, but no relationship is perfect. Once you make a choice, however, that person in some sense becomes "God's will" because he is the one to whom you make your vows. Life is *not* a cosmic treasure hunt in which God gleefully hides the one right person just to see if you can ferret him out.

I (Steve) do a live radio show every weekday. For one hour my colleagues and I take calls from all over the country and do our best to give them truth and insight. Recently, a call came from a woman that was identical to many other calls with the same concern. She had divorced her first husband, married a jerk, and now wanted to divorce him and go back to the first husband. Sorry. No matter how perfect husband number one was, it does not justify abandoning husband number two and going back to the first one. You see, whenever you make a mistake, God picks you up right there and lets you know He can work with the mistake and the circumstances you have chosen. You can't justify a break up because you might not have chosen the very one God had intended for you. Whoever you choose, once chosen, is the one God wants you to consider His choice. Because now that you are married, it is the one God wants for you.

We assume that people have the power to choose. In our culture adults choose with whom they partner for life. Parents may give input, but they do not dictate who our spouses will be. You can choose blindly or wisely. We believe there are guidelines that help us make good, godly, wise, less-risky choices. There are time-honored principles about life and relationships that are available to us when we choose a marriage partner. We may not value these qualities at first blush in a relationship, but they will be what makes someone "a keeper." We will go into those principals later in the book.

We also believe that being Ms. Right goes a long way in helping women find or attract Mr. Right. There are certain qualities for which a Mr. Right is looking. This fact does not mean women have to lose their distinctiveness, or become clones of some certain personality type. Within the wide variety of human personalities, however, there are basic human qualities that make for a more stable, safe, loving, and long-term relationship. Also, some personalities are attracted more to each other. A woman's understanding her own personality, and what type of person is apt to be attracted to her, is often very helpful.

Now that you are convinced it is okay to look, and you have realized that there is no *one* right person out there, what is the next step in finding Mr. Right? Well, being Ms. Right, of course.

CHAPTER 2

BEING MS. RIGHT FIRST

It is not enough to find Mr. Right. You must be the kind of woman Mr. Right would prefer. Some women complain that "there are no good men out there," but they never stop to examine if they are women who would appeal to a "good man." In this section we provide you with some insight into some pretty awful women. Our assumption is that if you were bright enough to be in a book store or online buying a book about relationships, you probably are not any of these women. However some of them may have a few characteristics that feel familiar to you. If that is the case, rather than deny being the type of woman we describe, just work on anything you have in common with her. Take heart. You can learn to do differently!

First off, understand that men do not like women who are looking for someone to fulfill, fix, or parent them. Men do not like being asked to do what only God can do (fulfill or fix you) or what your father should have done (parent you). While they may be flattered at first to be the object of your adoration, most men are not too keen on being put on a pedestal to be worshiped. They get tired of being the answer guy. Good men want to parent their children, not you.

Caring for someone is entirely different from taking care of someone. Incompetent adults, children, and infants need taking care of; adults who are capable of taking care of themselves expect others to do likewise. When we are ill or incapacitated in some manner, we all like and need some caretaking. That is only natural. But we come into the world alone, and we will go out of it alone. We are each responsible to our Creator for our own life.

Men (and here we mean *healthy* men) want women who like being cared about, but who know how to take care of themselves. Men want women who will partner with them, not drag them down. They want another adult, but not a mother. They want a companion, someone with whom to share life's ups and downs. They want a teammate, not an anchor.

Women who are sure of themselves, yet humble enough to take criticism, are far more attractive than the shrinking-violet types. A woman who is looking for her man to fulfill her, fix her, or parent her is going to be a drag on the relationship. Unable to carry her own weight, she clings to the man, expecting him to make her life meaningful, happy, full of contentment.

Second, a woman who has her priorities messed up will not attract Mr. Right. These women latch onto God, religion, and church not from devotion to God but as a means to an end: marriage. They see religious men as potentially good prospects, so they adopt a religious demeanor until they catch one. Imagine the poor guy's surprise after the wedding when he discovers his bride's faith is only as deep as the icing on the wedding cake.

Or perhaps these women are sincere in their faith but have a sort of twisted theology. According to their version of the gospel, they obey God, are good girls, and then God owes them. Owes them what? A husband, of course! Just another version of works theology, this approach is doomed to failure. This type of woman does not understand grace and is apt to be demanding not only of herself, but of others. She has high standards and expects herself and her man to live up to them. Think about how attractive that is.

Third, a woman who does not like herself is not going to attract a fine fellow. If you do not enjoy your own company, how do you expect anyone else to do so, especially a man? Other women sometimes put up with fellow females with low self-esteem because women are usually sympathetic and kind. They hate to see anyone left out. Yet even well-meaning friends get tired of propping someone else up all the time. Eventually, someone is apt to want to scream at her "Oh, for pity's sake, get a life!" Men are usually not so tolerant.

This last point, having strong self-esteem, is important enough that we want to explain more about it.

THE ROOTS OF GREAT SELF-ESTEEM

Many women think, *If only I had a date (boyfriend, husband) . . . then I would be happy.* This "if only" approach to life (which men use as much as women do) is faulty in that once achieved, the object of one's desire proves imperfect. Looking to another person for fulfillment (or wealth, power, position, or children) will never work. It is like pouring water through a sieve. The wire mesh gets wet indeed, but it does not hold the water. You must take responsibility for your own fulfillment.

But once you do, you will discover you cannot do it alone. You need people—not necessarily a man—who care about you. Other women can nurture and confront you, depending on your need. You may need a counselor to help you work out some areas that make you feel confused or empty. We think you need a church because there is so much to be gained from a healthy one. And we think you need to be developing a relationship with God. These are the things that lead to experiencing purpose and meaning and fulfillment.

Both of us have experienced the folly of basing our lives on anyone or anything else. You see, we each have been through marriage and divorce. Steve has been through some very good and some not so good times and has been married for almost 20 years. Meg has not remarried. During the last years of her marriage, she was so determined to "save" her drug-addicted husband that she refused to see that she wanted the marriage more than she wanted God. People come and go. Fame and glory are fleeting, at best. Money and power vanish in a minute. Children and friends, while loving, will fail us. No one can take the place of the Creator in a relationship. Of course people will use a thousand different methods to try, but nothing will come close to what a relationship with God will do for a person or a relationship.

God formed us in our mothers' wombs. We are not accidents. None of us is a mistake. But when we do not have a vital link to our Creator, we lose everything. We lose our purpose. We lose our role. We lose our identity. We flounder about like a fish on a dock. We rush from one thing to another, or one relationship to another, looking for meaning, looking for safety, looking for peace.

Does this sound like you? Have you lost your way? The Scripture says we are all like sheep who have wandered away from the Shepherd. How marvelous it is that the Shepherd, Jesus, knows us and goes out looking for us, to bring us home. We cannot find our own way. We cannot find our own purpose. He seeks us out. The Proverbs are a source of wisdom that cannot be matched anywhere. They tell us that there is before every person a very wide and pleasant road that looks so right but in the end brings death and destruction. If you are lost and on that wide road, there is a way back to the narrow path of purpose, fulfillment, and God's presence and love.

He yearns to find *you*. He waits for you to turn from the things or people to whom you have devoted yourself. He longs to give you all the fulfillment you need. My (Steve's) favorite scripture is Ephesians 3:20. It says that God will give you far more than you could ever hope for, imagine, or dream. I hope you believe that. I hope you can live everyday knowing there is a truly loving God who wants the very best for you in every way—a best that is beyond anything you could imagine.

True self-esteem can come only from experiencing our identity as creatures who are loved and formed in the image of our Creator. When we understand this love, our self-esteem will automatically soar. Too many women think they are only the roles they play (wife, sister, mom, friend) or the things they do (teach, train, clean, cook, work, study). Too many women think they are worthless because a dad, brother, mom, friend, or some man has rejected them. Some see their failures as too immense to overcome. And indeed, they are right. We cannot overcome our failures. Jesus is the Overcomer. He is the Victor. He takes our failures and brings good out of them, if we let go of them and give Him the place in our lives that He deserves.

And ladies, your shining heritage as women comes from your Creator. "Male and female he created them" (Gen. 1:27). Maleness alone does not reflect the glory and image of God. Together, male and female are the image of God. What a wonderful basis for identity and self-esteem! Women are not second-class citizens, no matter what some say. Women have a good and godly legacy as God's daughters.

In this superficial culture we are often defined by one-dimensional labels. You are either pretty or ugly. Smart or stupid. Clever or naive. Strong or weak. Often women wear these labels and subconsciously begin to fit them. No wonder self-esteem is such a problem. But we have a different perspective: every woman—ugly, pretty, smart, slow, wise, simple—no matter what her label, has secret powers that elevate her from a one-dimensional creature.

These secret powers are many. Too few women try to discover and use them. One is the power of a spiritual gift. Every Christian woman has a spiritually endowed skill that enables her to do certain things in certain areas that many others cannot. She might have the gift of administration. To her, details are comfortable, people are potential, and she enjoys organizing and evaluating a job that must be done. Some other woman has a gift of encouraging others. Others exercise a supernatural gift of discernment, and they can read a person's character instantly. There are many secret powers like this that provide a woman with special abilities. Every woman also has unique skills, talents, and interests that set her apart from others.

When a woman discovers all that she is and all the secret powers she possesses, self-esteem is no longer a problem. But today too few women are discovering how uniquely they are made and how empowered they are. If you want to be Ms. Right, you have to take that incredible journey toward discovering all of who you are. That journey begins by giving up some of the things that have kept you feeling safe and comfortable. Instead, you have to reach a point where you are willing to surrender everything you are to God and allow Him to mold you into something far beyond anything you could imagine possible. Then begin the journey by reading God's Word and discovering what the Holy Spirit is doing in your life today. Discover the supernatural spiritual gifts that have been entrusted to you. Discover God's truth and wisdom from Scripture and apply it to every area of your life. Do these things and you will be on a journey far greater than a journey of self discovery. You will be on a journey of self fulfillment.

WHO IS MS. RIGHT, ANYWAY?

Why, you are, if you want to be! What makes a woman "right" for a man? What appeals to a good man? What qualities do you need to develop if Mr. Right is to come your way? Here are ten to consider.

1. SHE IS APPROACHABLE

Do you make eye contact easily? Do you come across as open, warm, and non-threatening, even in a new situation? Nonverbal behaviors are important clues that give us the sense of whether or not someone is safe. Approachable gestures include eye contact, tilting the head, talking with the palms upward, shrugging the shoulders, smiling. Watch couples who are sitting at a social gathering. You will see some partners using gestures to shut each other out, such as folded arms, little or no eye contact, or not facing each other if one speaks.

Approachable people are good listeners. No one feels attracted for long to someone who talks a blue streak, especially about herself. Listening, on the other hand, demonstrates a capacity for empathy and understanding. Most people are desperate to be listened to sincerely. When a woman demonstrates interest by listening carefully and empathetically responding, she sends the message that she is a warm, welcoming person.

2. SHE IS GENUINE

Anyone can fake being approachable, warm, or interested for a while, but eventually the truth will come out, and the insincerity will be clear. Mr. Right wants someone who is genuinely interested in him as a person, not just in his money or sex appeal.

Long-term relationships require commitment and stamina, and only the real deal will work. Pretending to be someone you are not may be fun for the evening, but it will never lead to a lasting marriage commitment. Some people are incongruent (different inside from outside) because they are deceitful. Others are incongruent because they do not know who they are, and so they change their persona (the face they show others) according to the person they're with or the situation in which they find themselves. That is why knowing and liking oneself is crucial before jumping into the mating game. A secure person knows that she will be attracted to some people and not to others, and that likewise, some men will be attracted to her, and some will not. Confident in herself as a woman, she does not need to be fake just to keep a guy hanging around.

3. SHE IS ACCEPTING

Nothing turns a man off more than a critical woman. We are not talking here about constructive criticism. Women and men are capable of being analytical and discerning. This ability is a good thing—in its place. Misused in personal relationships, however, it can be deadly.

Critical women are never happy. The food is never good enough in the restaurant; the room is too cold or too hot; the movie was too juvenile or too violent; the card came too early or too late. No one likes a complainer. Men thrive on appreciation. They generally aim to please and like to be acknowledged for their effort, even if the end result is not perfect. A woman who can express gratitude for the thought behind an imperfect offering will be more attractive than one who is always complaining how he did not get it right.

Being accepting is more difficult for some than others. Certain personalities are geared toward "quality control," and the first thing they notice is how something or other does not meet the standard. And they feel often compelled to point it out. Other types, by contrast, have the ability to nurture, affirm, and build others up. It comes naturally for them to listen appreciatively, to compliment, to overlook small imperfections. They seem more able to see the big picture, both of the relationship and of the other person. They do not usually equate performance with acceptance.

Note: being accepting does not mean putting up with immoral or illegal behavior. Our society today is so open-minded that most of its brains have fallen out. *Tolerance* means allowing others to differ in thought or behavior. *Acceptance* means affirming or assenting to the behavior as okay or permissible. For example I may tolerate something in a friend that I would not accept in a marriage partner, such as smoking. Or I may neither tolerate nor accept certain behaviors, such as wife-beating. I can tolerate someone's belief, but I will not accept its being forced upon me. There is a difference between discerning that something is wrong but allowing for disagreement, and affirming something as valid or true. Our culture confuses tolerance with acceptance, much to our detriment as a society.

Mr. Right is looking for a woman who is appropriately—and appreciatively—accepting.

4. She Is Sexually Healthy and Interested

While no one is the perfect sexual partner, basic openness and a healthy interest are important. Unfortunately, some women have had negative sexual experiences. Perhaps they were raped or molested as a child, exposed to pornography, or taught that sex is evil or shameful or sinful. Some women are ignorant about the physical relationship between man and woman, even in this sexually saturated society. They do not understand their own bodies nor the dynamics of a physical relationship with a man. They may be reticent to talk about such matters because they do not want to appear forward or "loose."

It is crucial for a healthy relationship that both partners have a proper sexual education. This does not mean sexual experience, but rather information about male and female anatomy, the dynamics of sexual response for each partner, the mechanics of lovemaking, and the methods of birth control, if it is desired. A couple does not need to "try out" sex before marriage to see if they are well matched, but it is important to talk, talk, talk about expectations, level of desire, interest, fantasies, and previous exposure to sexual things.

5. She Is Spiritually and Ethically Committed

Ms. Right is someone who has a vibrant faith in God. While not necessarily a crusader, she is someone who knows right from wrong and is not afraid to stand up for it. She knows what and why she believes. Some people merely parrot what they learned as children, never actually studying a Bible to discover if it all makes sense. But Ms. Right takes spirituality seriously and wants to grow and learn from God and the Bible.

Ms. Right is teachable about spiritual matters. She recognizes that she herself does not have all the answers and is willing to listen to those who better understand the ways of God as she matures in her faith. Open to criticism, she is willing to listen to those who differ with her without being too defensive. She can hold her ground but is able to consider other points of view.

Ms. Right seeks to live what she believes. When she falls short in a relationship, she is able to ask and receive forgiveness from God, the other person, and herself. When wronged, she is able to consider God's perspective as she develops a response to a tough situation. She has a strong work ethic and practices honesty and integrity in all of her dealings. Ms. Right is someone who knows how to discipline her tongue enough to refrain from lashing out with remarks she would later regret. Not one to act one way on Sunday and differently the rest of the week, Ms. Right tries to apply her faith in the ethical arena of everyday life.

6. She Is Moderate

Ms. Right is someone who knows balance. Not given to excess, she enjoys life to the fullest but does not usually go overboard. She recognizes the principle that all things are given to us by God t... but she also recognizes that the pursuit of pleasure is not the be-all a... end-all of life. She is able to set boundaries with herself and others. That is, Ms. Right can say "yes" with enthusiasm when appropriate, and "no" just as emphatically when appropriate.

For example, Meg once had a tendency to withdraw and hibernate when going through a tough time. Her natural response was to get depressed and spend time alone, feeling sorry for herself. Over the years she has learned to counter this tendency with the assertiveness necessary to seek out the support she genuinely needs. She is moderate about her time alone.

Another example would be Jill. Jill was a people pleaser from the time she came out of her mother's womb. There was nothing she would not do for someone else. It consumed her, and every moment became a question of what was to be done for someone else. She sure made a lot friends that way. Or at least psuedo friends who used her until they were through with her and went on to the next person. It was only when she saw the use and abuse for what it was that she was able to moderate her people pleasing and replace it more with God serving.

Another example would be Margot, who knew she needed to get a handle on her sarcasm. Through counseling she learned that her caustic remarks were just a sideways kind of anger. This insight led her to be more honest with herself and others about what made her mad. Rather than sideswipe others with cutting remarks, Margot committed to speak directly and promptly to the person with whom she was angry. She was able to change from an abrasive, sarcastic woman to an assertive, proactive one who can speak sensitively and carefully.

Jeanne had to learn boundaries in another area: spending money. She recognized that she could not claim to put God first and have such an out-of-control area in her life. She obtained some credit counseling,

and worked her way out of debt. Jeanne
opping at an upscale store, she went to a fac-
buying new shoes every season, she made do
stead of seventy-dollar haircuts at the ritzy place
ac̲ ed for a reasonable one at Hair Is Us. Jeanne discovered tha̲ d just fine shopping at Wal-Mart instead of the
designer kitchen shop or the gourmet coffee store.

Jeanne began to see that the increased status she had felt when wearing designer clothes was just a superficial prop to her self-esteem. Instead of relying on fancy things to feel better, Jeanne began to take pride in herself and her ability to be more disciplined. All of this made her much more attractive to the kind of man with whom she wanted to connect.

Whether or not a person is moderate with food and drink reveals much. If a woman knows how to enjoy eating but is not obsessed with it (either by starving herself or being gluttonous), she is probably disciplined in other areas as well. A moderate woman respects herself enough to try to eat healthily and is not given to excess or compulsion.

Food is not the only substance that is used compulsively. In a day when at least one in ten people is chemically addicted, moderation (and in some cases abstinence) is indeed a virtue. Knowing one's limits and being able to set healthy boundaries for oneself is a sign of a mature person.

7. SHE IS EDUCATED AND ABLE TO SUPPORT HERSELF

While there may still be some men who are threatened by an educated woman, very few still espouse the view that women should be barefoot, pregnant, and in the kitchen. Even most conservative religious groups allow women to work outside the home, at least once the children are in school. Some men may struggle with wounded pride if their wives get more education or a bigger pay raise than they do. But most mature guys will admit this is only wounded ego, get beyond it, and rejoice in their wives' success.

Today, with many families needing two incomes to send kids to college, or to afford even a middle-class lifestyle, it is more and more necessary that a woman have a good education. With approximately half of marriages ending in divorce, even in the religious community, women must be prepared to take on financial responsibility for themselves and their children. We frequently hear stories of women who, once divorced, found themselves penniless and without adequate child support. Even women who have been married for decades are finding themselves out in the cold with an outdated or nonexistent education, and slim prospects job-wise. And were these cases not sobering enough, some women end up widowed far too early in life and need to be able to provide adequately for themselves and any children still at home.

While school may not be your first love, getting at least a high school diploma or a GED is a basic requirement for functioning in today's world. And it certainly is not going to make you unattractive!

Alyssa is a good example of how a lack of preparation can hurt. Married right out of college, she saw herself as a homemaker, mom, and wife. She worked in an office for a few years after marriage, when her husband was still in graduate school. When she got pregnant with her first child, she happily quit and began making their house more of a home. Four more kiddos followed in close succession, but Alyssa was content. Her husband, Frank, made an excellent salary and received great benefits. They had life insurance, so she was not concerned that she would ever need to work outside the home again.

Then disaster struck. Out of the blue, or so it seemed, Frank began to experience various neurological symptoms that scared both of them. After extensive testing, the doctors finally diagnosed him with Parkinson's disease, and both of them were stunned. Frank became

depressed as the disease progressed more rapidly than they had anticipated. Within two years he was wheelchair bound and able to work
only part time. The kids were in private school, and soon the family's
savings dwindled. Alyssa had to go back to work.

Her college degree had been in art history, and she had not learned
all the new computer skills that even fifth-graders now have. Devastated,
she became depressed and ended up requiring antidepressant medica-
tion and therapy. Not only did she have to retrain, but she had to
assume more and more responsibility at home as Frank's condition
deteriorated. How she wished she had taken her dad's advice and at
least minored in education so she could have fallen back on teaching
when she needed work. Suddenly she had to make up for lost time.

The core issue here is not just being able to provide for the family
if your husband gets sick. It is a matter of you respecting yourself and
your husband respecting you. If he knows you can make it on your
own, he will respect you more. The condition that leads to many sor-
rows for a woman is desperation. Desperate women fall prey to
threats and live their lives in fear. You need to have experience and
education that allow you to be confident in life and in yourself. The
more independent you are, the less likely you will ever have to be
totally independent.

8. She Is Wise

Who would be attracted to a fool? Probably only another fool!
While all of us do unwise things at times, we should pay attention
when we see a behavior repeated over and over again. Sometimes we
think our love will win the foolish person over, or change him in some
fundamental way. Or we think we can act foolishly now, even repeatedly, and somehow, some way, we will be able to rise above the consequences of our foolishness.

What does it mean to be a wise person? Wisdom consists of

knowledge plus perspective. The Bible says that knowledge alone just makes a person feel superior to others. Knowledge without perspective can be neutral in theory, but once it is applied, perspective is needed. For example, as a police officer, a person will learn how to handle a gun. Unapplied, that knowledge is neither good nor bad. If used without perspective, however, that same knowledge can become an evil thing: knowing *how* to shoot is one thing, knowing *when* to shoot is a matter of perspective. The wise person has both knowledge and perspective.

If you are honest, you will recognize pretty readily why a Mr. Right would not be attracted to an unwise or foolish woman. Only Mr. Fool would find such a woman attractive. Respect for one another; genuine regard for another's welfare; being fair and even-tempered; being prudent and careful with one's time, talent, and resources—all these things and more are characteristics of a wise person. Yet today, we see them less and less in everyday circumstances. Crudeness, rudeness, and just plain stupidity are touted as the way to be cool. Callousness, hardheartedness, and self-absorption are all promoted at the expense of what would be wise in a long-term relationship.

The foolish lasts for a moment; the wise will stand for a lifetime. If you would prefer a wise man to a foolish one, would it not be wise to grow in wisdom? What could you possibly lose?

9. She Is Playful, Fun, and Relaxed

Ever try to have a nice time with a sourpuss? Think about the last party you went to and who was the biggest party pooper. Who was always complaining, griping about the food, the decor, the lighting, the drinks, the people, the noise? Who could never take a joke or a little teasing? Who sat in the corner looking so deadly serious, you thought he had fallen asleep or died sitting up? Not real attractive, huh?

A mature person knows that there is a time for everything: a time to sow, a time to reap; a time to laugh and a time to cry; a time to work and a time to play. In the Old Testament, God proscribed that His people, the Jews, have many festivals and holidays. Why? Because God made us for both joy and sorrow. Life is hard enough. If you cannot laugh at least at yourself, you are in trouble. A wise person balances her time so she is not lopsided: all work and no play does make Jane dull.

Being able to have fun does not mean being super-extroverted or the life of the party. It means being able to relax, not take life too seriously, and be silly once in a while.

One of things that makes a relationship special is the shared history of funny events: in fact, one of the key components of a marriage that lasts is a common sense of humor. You have to be able to laugh at yourself and each other to survive. You have to be willing to retrace the steps when you looked the most ridiculous, said the most stupid things. And you have to be able to laugh at your own family as well as his. Grandma losing her false teeth down the garbage disposal; Uncle Harry getting his arm stuck in the hide-a-bed couch; little Janey running down the path to the lake, stark naked, determined to have a swim, not a bath! All these precious moments are what tie us together as human beings. They form a foundation of reference and connection that keeps us together when the last thing we want to do is be connected.

Someone who knows how and when to laugh and can evoke laughter in others is always attractive. Having a good sense of humor is an invaluable virtue. Some of us may be more witty than others, but all of us can cultivate the childlike attitude necessary to have fun.

10. SHE IS ACTIVE

What do we mean? Well, at least, we mean Ms. Right is not a couch potato! What kinds of activity do we recommend? Any and all kinds—physical, mental, social, ethical, moral. Even people who are physically challenged are active in sports these days. No one needs to be on the sidelines. We can all do *something* with our bodies. If you are not active physically, see your doctor and find out what exercise is best for you. Start slowly and try various things. Find a routine that suits you and one you enjoy.

Maybe you aren't up to jogging two miles, but you could walk fifteen minutes a day with your dog. Or run up and down the stairs in the hall at work on your break. Or swim, ski, ride a bike, row a boat, dance. Many don't realize it, but gardening has many benefits of other forms of exercise, and you get to see some beautiful plants and eat some fresh food as an added reward for your efforts. Develop a hobby that involves movement: bicycling for thirty minutes a week, walking dogs for people who are away on vacation, or helping handicapped children at recess. Once you start to move, you will wonder why it took you so long to get off the couch.

Develop active mental hobbies: learn a language, develop computer skills, write poetry, do crossword puzzles or other word teasers. Anything that stimulates the brain, like word puzzles, also makes you a more interesting person, better able to carry on a fascinating conversation with someone you are attracted to. Join a local community chorus or a drama club. Memorizing lines and tunes is a great way to keep your brain humming.

Learn about other cultures. Travel to new places. Try new foods. Learn to cook or dance or sew or fix cars. Lifelong learning is the key to mental alertness. No one is attracted to a deadhead. Determine to be sharp as a tack and you will always be an interesting person.

Socially, if you are inactive, get with it. What do we mean? Well, for one thing, you will not find Mr. Right coming down your chimney like Santa, so you have to get out of the house! Find some people who make you laugh and hang with them. Start having fun. Ask friends who are married to invite you over when their single male friends are coming too. *Do* something. Be somebody. Get noticed!

RATE YOURSELF

Okay, how are you doing? Are you well on the way to being Ms. Right, or do you need some help? Here's the list again. Rate yourself from 1 (hardly ever) to 10 (always). Go back and reread any section of which you are unsure.

Ms. Right is

1. Approachable
2. Genuine
3. Accepting
4. Sexually healthy and interested
5. Spiritually and ethically committed
6. Moderate
7. Educated and able to support herself
8. Wise
9. Playful, fun, and relaxed
10. Active

Scoring:

0–10   You need some help *now!* Get some counseling as soon as possible!

11–20   You have a ways to go and could use encouragement.

21–30   You are obviously trying and need some support.

31–40   You are moving in the right direction!

41–50   You are almost halfway there! Get some feedback to see what is holding you back.

51–60   You are making definite strides. Keep plugging away and look for a good mentor.

61–70   You are becoming an attractive person. You feel happier and more confident.

71–80   You have a lot to be proud of. Keep up the good work!

81–90   You are a gem!

91–100 Wow! Are you sure you were honest?

If you are brave enough, ask your mom or your best friend to rate you too. See if your scores agree.

Peter Drucker is a man who possesses much wisdom. Mr. Drucker is probably the most widely read and respected management and organizational guru alive today. The secular world beats a path to his doorstep, and he just happens to be a great Christian also. He said that one of the most self-destructive traits of people is the desire for the quick fix. We all want one. We want everything now rather than later. Delayed gratification is a lost art. We pace in front of the microwave because it does not get the job done fast enough.

Remember that becoming Ms. Right is a process. You can't go from being a shy, inactive girl who has been knocked around and used to being a respected, wise woman in one month. It is going to take time for you to become Ms. Right. It is never too early to start on the process. It is also never too late. Decide now that you are willing to do the tough work it will take to become the woman of some man's dreams.

CHAPTER 3

WHAT *YOU* MUST DO
TO FIND MR. RIGHT

You mean there's more? Yep! As you probably know, unless you are living in a terminal state of denial, it takes more than just becoming Ms. Right to find Mr. Right. It lays the foundation to all that follows, but there is a lot more to be done. We want you to have the best chance possible of finding this man, so we have compiled eleven steps we think are important to consider. While some of these may overlap with our suggestions for becoming Ms. Right, they are worth emphasizing.

Read on.

ELEVEN ESSENTIAL STEPS FOR
FINDING MR. RIGHT

1. MAKE THE MOST OF YOUR APPEARANCE

Like it or not, people do judge a book by its cover. You may not be Miss America, but you probably could look better than you do. Most of us can, and all of us need to take stock once in a while. Styles, makeup, haircuts that worked when we were fifteen or twenty-one or thirty may not work now. Maybe you have a "problem figure." Do some research. Get some help. Most department stores now have consultants who are trained to help customers find wardrobes that are attractive for their body type. All kinds of books are being published about color and style. You can find out what helps you look your best. Every woman has a chance to improve her appearance if she wants to do so.

Now listen: in talking about this, we are not succumbing to superficial standards. As tough as it is, this is reality. There are some singles who rationalize being obese, not wearing makeup, or ignoring their hairstyles by saying that they want a man who loves what they are on the inside. We understand the sentiment, but did you ever notice how the valuable stuff has a nice wrapper also?

You do not have to be a beauty to find Mr. Right. But you do have to respect yourself enough to do the most with what you have when it comes to physical appearance.

2. Know What You Are Looking For

Do not take the first fellow that passes by just because he is interested. Do not end up being a desperate dame. With scholarships, grants, loans, and awards available to women in many areas, no woman need be undereducated and hence not self-sufficient. Sure, independence takes hard work, and it is easier to assume some knight in shining armor is coming to your rescue, but marrying someone just because you cannot support yourself financially is a bad idea.

Set a standard for yourself. Do not settle. Find someone who meets or exceeds your standards, not falls beneath it. With what kind of man would you enjoy spending the rest of your life, parenting and raising children, growing older? If you do not know now what type of man you want and need, how will you ever find him?

3. TAKE YOUR TIME

Rome wasn't built in a day and neither are healthy relationships. Besides knowing what type of man is suitable for you, you must not rush into anything. It takes at least three months to get over the infatuation stage in a dating relationship, so any decisions made in that time period may be regrettable later. You need time and patience to truly get to know someone.

Do not let friends or relatives hurry you along. After all, you will be the one marrying the man, not them. If you need more time, it cannot hurt to wait.

In order to evaluate a relationship wisely, you need to see the man under many different stresses and in many different settings. If you have known him only at church, on the job, on a cruise, or at the gym, you do not genuinely know him. Seeing him when he is sick, in a bad mood, in extreme pain, or suffering a deep loss are all important experiences you should have before making a marital decision. Those events take time. They usually do not happen in three months.

4. KEEP GROWING

Just like a plant, humans can keep growing until the day they die. Lifelong learning is not something good only for your career. Having an open mind and being willing to grow in relational skills, emotional development, and social graces will speed you on your way to happiness, with or without a man in your life. And you will be all the more attractive too!

Challenge yourself to grow in areas where you are weak or less than perfect. Unsure what that would mean? Often psychological testing can give insight on personality and one's strengths and weaknesses. Perhaps a school counselor or a New Life Clinic psychologist (1–800–NEW LIFE) could help you get the kind of testing you would find insightful. Getting counseling is often a productive way to help yourself keep growing personally. As you develop confidence in yourself, you will become more and more attractive.

Understand that people seek out a counselor for many reasons. At New Life Clinics, we have been providing counseling from a Christian perspective since 1988. It is interesting to note a change in the trend. In the eighties, most people who sought counseling were desperate and needed help with some major problem. That is not the case today. Most counseling now is for character development. People who come in now often know where they are and that they need a bit of a boost to move forward. They want more. Our encouragement to you is to want more and get whatever help you need to grow personally, spiritually, and relationally.

5. KNOW AND STICK TO YOUR SEXUAL STANDARDS

Mr. Right is not looking for an easy woman. Despite the plethora of sexual input in our culture today, not everyone is having sex before marriage. Men may be willing to mess around with women for a while, but when they are serious about marriage, they do not like "used goods." It may be hypocritical, but it is a reality. Men who are the Mr. Rights of the world are looking for women who are moral, chaste, and able to be faithful. (Of course, Mr. Right must uphold the same standards of fidelity and faithfulness.)

Not only is sexual promiscuity stupid behavior, in this day and age it is life-threatening behavior. Many times women make a mistake when they assume that by giving a man sex, they will receive the love and commitment they long for in return. In reality, most men will promise anything just to get sex. Once they are satisfied physically, they quickly forget about any professions they may have made. Love and sex are not the same thing, and a wise woman does not confuse them.

6. KEEP YOUR SENSE OF HUMOR

Nothing is more unattractive than a grouch. A smile is winsome, a frown is repugnant. If you take yourself and your single status too seriously, you will drive away those men who might have been interested. Being able to laugh at yourself is a sign of maturity and makes any woman someone others like to be around. Sometimes dating and all the stuff that goes with it just gets downright silly. If you can laugh instead of cry, you will be better off in the long run, no matter what happens with a particular relationship.

7. ACCEPT YOURSELF AND OTHERS WITH GRACE

We are all fallible. Men and women, as individuals and sexes, have strengths and weaknesses. Sometimes our culture swings in an anti-female or anti-male direction. We need to resist these forces of prejudice and accept one another as partners in God's creation. Both women and men reflect the image of God. In fact, as we stated in the last chapter, that image is not fully reflected by either sex separately. That is why God said that it was not good for Adam to be alone, and He created Eve.

Neither sex has a monopoly on God's image, grace, or blessing. The more we understand the value of one another, the more we will find ourselves able to get along. You are special and created in the image of God just as much as any man is. Yet God has given women partners with whom to reflect His glory: the men of our world. Accepting ourselves and others as human and fallible rather than seeing them as "the enemy" will ultimately only make us more attractive.

8. LOOK IN THE RIGHT PLACES!

Mr. Right is probably closer than you think. As we recommended in the last chapter, get out there and find him! Take classes, join a softball league, volunteer, join community groups (Kiwanis, Big Brothers/Big Sisters, summer theater, local choirs) as well as alumni groups, charity fund-raising groups, or political parties. Become an emergency medical technician or join the volunteer fire department. Offer to help out with a local Boy Scout or Cub Scout troop (you never know which little boy has an eligible dad). Exercise classes, dances, church outings, camping programs, and adult education opportunities can all be venues for meeting a future spouse. Step outside your comfort zone and take a few risks. Jump out of an airplane! You never know whom you might meet in sky-diving class.

Church can be another place to meet someone of like values and mind-set. But do not let the fact that you met the man in church entice you to put your common sense aside and jump in blindly. Even at church you can meet a deceiver or a con artist, and there are some who specialize in looking for vulnerable women at places of worship. Use the same guidelines for someone at church that you would for someone you meet at a party or a cousin's wedding. Check out "references," that is, get to know who knows him well. Ask around. Do not be shy—find out all you can. Not everything you hear will be true, perhaps, but it at least will keep you alert. He may be a fellow believer, but he may or may not be Mr. Right for you.

Remember, Mr. Right is much more apt to be hanging out in some kind of productive place rather than at a bar or dance club.

A word about the Internet: many people today are touting the value and/or peril of this millennial phenomenon. For example, the August 28, 2000 issue of *U.S. News & World Report* had as its cover story "The Dark Side of the Internet: I. D. Theft, Child Porn, Securities Swindles, Stalking, Credit Fraud, Adoption Scams." And the title is just the beginning. Close to 150 million Americans are hooked up to the Net. While most people are aware of the wonderful side of the Net—information access, instant communication, video and audio access, e-books, Web pages on every topic you can think of—most people are not aware of how wide and deep the dark side really is.

The bottom line is, use extreme caution with the Web as a meeting place (more on this in Chapter 11).

9. TELL YOUR FRIENDS AND FAMILY

Do not be shy! Let your friends and family know the kind of man you need and want. Let your desire to find Mr. Right be known by those who love and care for you. Many times successful couples report that they met through friends and family. In fact, some report that the best place to meet your future spouse is at a relative or friend's wedding! So rather than staying home and avoiding weddings, let yourself be seen by those who could introduce you to a wonderful someone. Be open to suggestions about how to make yourself more attractive. Honestly consider comments about someone who may not look like Mr. Right at first glance but who could just be hiding under that sheepish grin or scruffy beard!

10. BE HOSPITABLE

Host parties, dinners, and other social occasions. You do not have to be a gourmet cook to make people feel comfortable in your home. You never know which friend will bring a friend or a cousin who just happens to be in town. Make your house the place people want to come visit. You do not need a giant swimming pool or a huge TV screen. People today are looking for community, for caring, and for a sense of belonging. You can be the catalyst that brings them together, and in the process find your Mr. Right.

11. BE GENUINE, HONEST, AND APPROACHABLE

As we mentioned in Chapter 2, being genuine and approachable will make you a safe person to be around. Men are looking for someone who will not emotionally castrate them. They need to feel secure that you will not be a critical mother figure.

You can be honest but not brutal. Tact is a wonderful quality that makes any person more approachable and easy to like. If you are gruff, sullen, or silly you will be more apt to put men off than attract them. Ask your mom or aunt or mentor if you are as approachable as you might be. Getting feedback on your style can be scary at first but very useful in the long run.

Now, if you look at this list and say that out of the eleven there are only about three that you possess or could actually accomplish, that is okay. Go and make the most of those three. Work at them, develop them, do whatever you can to bring those steps to life. Those three may become so powerful that they overcome the fact that the other eight are a bit lacking.

You do not have to be perfect to find Mr. Right. Take what you have and do with it what you can. The mere fact that you are in the process of growth, development, and improvement will make you more interesting, complex, and attractive.

CHAPTER 4

THE WOMAN EVERY MR. RIGHT IS LOOKING FOR

What does a man want in a woman, anyway? Do all men look for the same things? Does Mr. Right's wish list differ from Mr. Wrong's? In our book *Avoiding Mr. Wrong*, we devoted a good bit of space to this question. Suffice it to say that the goals Mr. Right has significantly differ from those of Mr. Wrong. Mr. Right is not interested primarily in a "good time" girl. He is not looking for a bed partner. He is looking for a life partner. He is not looking for a "party girl." He is looking for a relationship.

MS. RIGHT DEFINED

1. A WOMAN WHO IS INTERESTED IN A RELATIONSHIP

What do we mean? What is a relationship between two human beings of the opposite sex supposed to be like? Is it one person merging with another person, giving up his or her identity? Is one person in control, the other totally passive? Is it a competition—a contest to see who is smarter, sexier, more productive financially?

While the word *relationship* has probably been used to describe any of these interactions (and more), none of these describes what we mean. To us, and we hope to you, being in relationship means an intimate (in the broadest sense), committed, equal, consistent, and faithful interaction between two people of the opposite sex, which eventually leads to a permanent covenant in marriage.

We were created to be in relationship, first with God, then with each other, and then with the world God made as its caretakers. This shared authority and intimacy are the biblical ideal for marriage. For this reason, a man leaves his father and mother and is joined in unity with his wife.

When Mr. Right is looking for a relationship, then he is looking for a mate, a partner, a person suited to him who is willing to be united in purpose and authority, to carry out human responsibility here on earth. He may not articulate it in such a fancy way, but that is his longing. He is looking for a closeness that is fundamental to our humanness. He is not looking for a one-night stand, a mere sexual release of tension, a good time in "the sack." Sexual fulfillment, he understands, is part of marriage, not dating.

Therefore, Ms. Right knows that being in a relationship is for keeps. It is a sacred responsibility, just as producing and parenting a child is. Ms. Right has her priorities straight and is not about to put the "horse before the cart." To her, marriage means the promise to share life together in every way, forever. It is a costly and precious commitment, not to be entered into lightly. She anticipates its joys and privileges but does not kid herself about its responsibilities. She has a woman's perspective rather than an adolescent's view; she aspires to what is noble and sacred, not just self-fulfilling.

2. A WOMAN WHO IS LOVING

Ms. Right wants to serve, love, and bring out the best in her husband. Where Ms. Wrong wants attention and satisfaction for herself, Ms. Right seeks to put her husband first. There is a name for the kind of love Ms. Right wants to emulate; in the New Testament it is the word *agape*. Agape love goes beyond erotic love and beyond the kindly affection we see between a child and a parent or between two good friends. It denotes much more than mere feeling; it shows itself best in actions rather than words. It is the kind of love that makes a lifelong relationship work.

The woman we just described sounds pretty ideal. Can anyone really qualify? While no man or woman can perfectly love in the agape sense, the Bible makes it clear that with God's assistance, through the power of the Spirit, we can be transformed and enabled to love beyond ourselves. So Mr. Right is looking for someone who aims high yet forgives herself and others; when failure comes (and it will), she can continue the relationship.

Ms. Right expects the same unconditional love and acceptance from Mr. Right that she offers to him. In essence, she is the safe person in his life. She is someone with whom he can be honest, genuine, congruent. She is not going to criticize or chop him off at the knees every time he does not meet her expectations. She is humble enough, and has enough of a sense of humor, that she can offer understanding and perspective without muttering condescending remarks. She is a loving woman in every sense.

3. A WOMAN WHO IS WHOLE

Mr. Right is looking for a woman who knows herself, her needs, her wants, and her priorities but is willing to put these aside when necessary for the good of the relationship or the family. He expects no less of himself and wants their relationship to be as reciprocal as possible, given their differing personalities, gifts, and abilities. Only a control freak would want a one-sided relationship where one person gives and the other receives. Mr. Right is looking for a woman who has a life of her own. Mr. Right is not seeking a parasite. He wants a partner, a teammate, a companion, not someone who will suck the life out of him. In short, he wants a woman who is whole.

Marriage is not two half-people coming together to make one whole person. Rather it is two whole people uniting for a common purpose: to double their resources. Mr. Right is looking for someone who can contribute and who will appreciate his contributions. He wants a woman who knows her strengths as well as her weaknesses. She is not afraid to lean on him, but she can also give support when it is needed.

4. A Woman Who Is Stable

No Mr. Right wants a long-term relationship with a flake. He is looking for a partner who will be an asset to his life, not a liability. All of us have had periods of instability of one sort or another: financial, emotional, spiritual, relational, physical. We all have our ups and downs. But what Mr. Right is looking for is a woman who has dealt with her issues to the best of her ability. She balances her own check-book and is disciplined in her spending. She knows how to modulate her moods and keep her temper under control. She does not let herself be dominated by either her feelings or obsessive thinking.

This woman is flexible and able to see where she tends to be rigid. She is willing to receive feedback from him and others about her progress in becoming a more stable person. She recognizes her liabilities as a person and has put a lot of effort into changing them into assets.

Again, we all get wobbly from time to time due to physical illness, accidents, crises, loss, or disabilities. We all need support and reassurance sometimes. But if you suffer from a long history of emotional instability, *work on it*. Get some help. See if there is a competent Christian counselor in your area who can help you. Deal with your issues now, and you will only improve your chances of attracting Mr. Right.

5. A WOMAN WHO IS A COMPANION

Mr. Right is looking for a woman who understands his need to be with her. Men value doing things with a woman. They may just be going to the hardware store, but they like having you along. They may not say anything all the way there, but they are still gratified for your companionship.

Remember, the male definition of "being with" does not necessarily include talking. He gets the same warm, fuzzy feeling from being in the house with you (even if you are in the attic and he is in the basement) or at the store with you that you get when he looks you directly in your eyes and tells you how much you mean to him. In his mind your being with him, each accomplishing whatever you are doing, means *We're a team, she's with me, she is on my side, this is our house.* Many men feel cheated after marriage when their wives do not want to go places and do things with them. Such wives seem to think, *Well, I am with him at home now, so I don't have to go to the hardware store with him.* They miss the point that one of the things husbands treasure simply is being with them.

Part of this partnership involves hobbies. The woman Mr. Right wants has activities she likes doing and he does not. However, some will include him for a very important reason: recreational companionship is one of the crucial bonding ingredients in marriage. While all of us have different skills and abilities, if *all* the things we enjoy exclude our spouse by their very nature, the relationship is in trouble. We have only so many hours a day to "play," and if all the pleasures in our lives exclude our spouse, we will begin to value being away from them more than being with them.

The same goes for the things we devote our leisure time to doing. If we play golf only with people from work, and do not do anything fun with our spouse, he or she will begin to associate us with all the difficult stuff in life and associate coworkers with the good, fun, pleasant things. Guess where he or she will want to spend time?

A word of caution: A woman should never pretend to like something simply to please her boyfriend or husband. It is one thing not to be crazy about something yet participate in it because you want to be with him, but it is altogether another thing to pretend you like football, hockey, or bowling if you despise it. Most of us have activities we are enthused about doing and activities we can enjoy but are not devoted to doing. These are the things recreational companionship should focus upon: the hobbies in which both of you find pleasure. It is not fair to expect someone to love what he dislikes simply because you love it.

This is not as hard as it sounds. It would be the rare couple who cannot find something that they both like. Most of the time, when people say that they "have nothing in common," they either have never made the effort to build a mutual companionship, or there is so much emotional distance between them that they are not able to enjoy anything together.

6. A Woman Who Laughs

Mr. Right is looking for a woman with a good sense of humor. She is able to take a joke, make a joke, and laugh at a joke. She knows how to have fun without resorting to sick, dirty, or hurtful humor. She knows the difference between funny and sarcastic. She never uses jokes to cut a man to ribbons, especially in front of others. Her humor uplifts and cheers those around her. Whether her wit is dry or silly, she knows how to use humor to encourage her man. She is tactful and able to get her point across without being cruel.

7. A WOMAN WHO IS A HOMEMAKER

Mr. Right is not looking for a housekeeper, he is looking for a homemaker. Men look to women to create the home atmosphere. Some attribute this ability to a "nesting instinct." Whatever its source, most women seem to have a knack and a need to make a home. Decorating, creating, fixing up, planting gardens, and adding beauty, while not strictly feminine skills, are usually practiced by the woman in a family.

Women are also often the family social engineers in that they are in charge of keeping everyone on track and at the right place at the right time. Creating a family life, social activities, and a community of friends is usually delegated to—or taken on by—the woman.

Even when Mr. Right is the more extroverted person, he may look to his wife to be the one who organizes and arranges the hospitality they want to offer others in their home. This can be a burden to the more introverted woman, who may need to enlist his support to do the up-front hosting activities while she does the behind-the-scenes arrangements with which she is more comfortable. Homemaking, socializing, and entertaining are all skills many men value in women they marry.

So is child-rearing. The old sayings, "The hand that rocks the cradle rules the world" and "Behind every great man stands a great woman," contain some truth! Obviously, most men are looking for a woman who wants to be the mother of his children. Of course men still have a responsibility to parent, but most want their children to have a mother who is active in their lives.

By the way, not agreeing on the desire to have children is a significant danger signal for a couple considering marriage. While marriage is more than procreation, bearing and raising children is one of the strong biological, spiritual, and psychological reasons people marry. Couples should be sure they are on the same page in this regard before they marry.

If you like making home a fun, relaxing, and welcoming place for family and friends, Mr. Right will find you very appealing.

8. A WOMAN WHO COMMUNICATES

No one likes to try to read other people's minds. For one thing it is impossible to do, and for another, it is a pain in the neck to try. Mr. Right wants a woman who communicates clearly, honestly, and succinctly. Men do not like to second-guess what is going on in women's heads. They value ladies who can speak their minds in a loving, non-critical manner. When a woman is skilled at "speaking the truth in love" (Eph. 4:15), she has developed a quality that is very attractive to men.

Men, whether they like it or not, have fragile egos. They are easily hurt by criticism and quickly feel rejected or wounded by hurtful remarks. It is not that they want flattery or lies. They want the truth, but they value a woman who can say it in a way that leaves their dignity intact and allows them to save face.

Being blunt is not the same thing as being truthful. Even horses react better when they are led to water rather than dunked in it. Smart men want to benefit from constructive criticism. They recognize that "two heads are better than one" and that they need a woman's perspective. Mr. Right knows he does not have all the answers and that he can use some supportive guidance now and again. He does not want a boss but a fellow traveler. He wants to benefit from a woman's wisdom. But he hates to have to guess what it is!

9. A WOMAN WHO IS AN AFFIRMER

Isn't it fun to be with someone who appreciates you? You feel so good, you can hardly wait to see him again! You miss him when he is gone and long to hear his voice. You feel built up, encouraged, strengthened by his very presence. You come to count on his support.

Men are not different from women in this regard. We all need appreciation. We all need to feel wanted, valuable, desired for what we have to offer. Men and women do differ in what they appreciate about each other, but both sexes need acknowledgment. Women long to be understood and honored for who they are as women. Men often focus more on being thanked for what they do, for how hard they work, or for the effort they put forth. Mr. Right is looking for a woman who knows how to be appreciative—not fawning and manipulative, but genuinely grateful.

In our society, we have forgotten that women can be grateful without being subservient. We have become so focused on our "rights" that we have lost perspective on the graciousness of giving and receiving. Appreciating what someone does for you and honoring him for doing it does not make you a lackey or a slave or a lower form of life. It just means you recognize how pleasurable it is not to have to do everything yourself. Yes, you could open the door for yourself, but it sure is nice when your friend does it for you. Yes, you could change your flat tire or fill the gas tank, but it is nice to find it done for you when you go to use the car. Yes, you could parent your child all by yourself, but who would want to?

When you do something kind, nice, or uplifting for someone else, it does not make him obligated to you in some sick manner, and when he reciprocates it is not demeaning to be appreciative. Mr. Right just wants to be appreciated the same way you do.

10. A WOMAN WHO IS A LOVER

One very important quality Mr. Right is looking for is a woman who is open to being a great lover. Sexual inhibition is deadly to a marriage. This is not to say that a woman needs to be experienced. One of the big lies in our society today is that you have to have sex with someone before the wedding to make sure you are compatible. Rubbish! One of the things that forms a bond between two people during the first part of the marriage is either working through sexual incompatibility or improving on the sexual compatibility that is there. The level of sex drive will be different at different times. Rarely is there a real live "plumbing problem," but it happens. When it does it is an opportunity to grow together through the process. What makes for a poor sexual relationship is not a lack of expertise or experience but rather a lack of respect, tenderness, and openness to the beauty of the sexual area of life.

Some women have been hurt sexually through incest, rape, or brutality in a previous relationship. Some have never experienced a man's being nice to them, much less being a gentle lover. Some women confuse sex with love and assume if they give the one they will get the other. Some women have been taught that sex is dirty, a duty, or evil. These women are sadly misinformed and missing out on one of God's best blessings in life.

If you find yourself in one of these categories, *get help* before you get married. Explore your attitudes and feelings about sex with a competent Christian therapist who understands morality and sexuality. Also talk honestly about these issues with Mr. Right, if you find him.

The results of incest, rape, and sexual molestation are serious wounds that need serious healing. Many men have felt cheated to discover that their wives do not enjoy sex because of some tragedy in the past which has not been healed, and their wives are missing out on an important intimacy God planned for married couples.

Ms. Right understands that men approach sexuality differently from the way women do. She does not assume Mr. Right understands her view of it and communicates about it clearly and gently. She never chooses instead to "fake it" or conceal the truth from him.

Mr. Right is looking for a woman who will be open to new sexual ideas and experiences. She will understand—and anticipate—that sex is a lifelong and joyous growth experience within the safety of marriage.

So, here is the short list. Mr. Right is looking for a woman who is

- interested in a relationship.
- loving.
- whole.
- stable.
- a companion.
- able to laugh.
- a homemaker.
- a communicator.
- an affirmer.
- a lover.

Know that you can grow and become the type of woman any Mr. Right would be proud to have as his wife. Help is available. Others have aimed high and made it, and so can you! Just be sure you do not expect perfection of yourself or him. Rigid perfectionism makes any potential Ms. Right into Ms. Wrong.

PART II

IDENTIFYING MR. RIGHT

CHAPTER 5

A MAN OF CHARACTER, FAITH, AND PURPOSE

Some of us were fortunate enough to grow up in families where the father, uncles, brothers, and/or grandfathers were examples of what Mr. Right could be. Not everyone is so fortunate. Some of us had dads or male relatives who were absent, neglectful, or even evil. In case you are one who has never known a good man, we will examine the qualities you will want to look for in Mr. Right.

A MAN OF CHARACTER

Bud is an amazing person. He is eighty-four years old and has been married sixty years to his wife, Lorena. They had six kids and raised them in modest circumstances through the boom of the fifties and the turbulent sixties. They went through all the typical stuff: chicken pox, measles, sibling rivalry, broken bones, tight budgets, hand-me-downs, and assembling tricycles on Christmas Eve. They also experienced the unusual: the Hong Kong flu epidemic, the introduction of the polio vaccine, the fluoridation of the water supply, Vietnam, and the assassinations of President Kennedy, his brother Bobby, and Martin Luther King.

Bud and Lorena went to church, taught their kids the Ten Commandments, and remained committed to their faith even when their son Tim died in Vietnam. They lived and laughed their way through their daughter's hippie wedding out in a field in Minnesota, poignant good-byes when their middle son and his family left for the mission field in Africa, and a bout with breast cancer when Lorena was fifty years old.

Bud worked as a machinist at a big aircraft plant near their home. He rose in the ranks and eventually became a supervisor. Bud's fellow workers trusted him because of his honesty, integrity, and fairness. Not one to let his temper get the best of him, Bud always sought solutions that met everyone's needs as much as possible. His simple faith in God kept him focused on what mattered to him, and he was known as a loyal friend, faithful husband, and caring dad.

This is surprising when you consider Bud's roots. His dad was an alcoholic, and Bud grew up in a rough part of town, where other Eastern European immigrant families had settled. His mom and dad fought bitterly over his drinking, and his Mom took in laundry to supplement his dad's meager and somewhat sporadic income. Bud's grandmother, who barely spoke English, had come to live with them when Bud was about six years old, so he had to sleep on the couch in the living room. Bud had seven brothers and sisters, and because he was the oldest, he was expected to work after school to bring in supplemental income. His uncle got him a job hauling trash at the local machine shop when he was a teenager. Later he became an apprentice and learned the trade firsthand.

What is remarkable about Bud is his faithfulness. Rain or shine, good or bad, Bud just keeps going along, faithfully fulfilling his responsibilities. You can see it throughout his life, but especially in the way he cares for Lorena. When she developed Alzheimer's disease, Bud could have put her in a nursing home; he could easily afford it. He could have asked one of his kids to take her. He could have been resentful, bitter, nasty. Yet he chose to take on her care, and is tender, kind, and sweet to Lorena. He talks to her as if she understands every word he says. He lovingly bathes her, changes her diapers, washes her clothes, feeds her, puts her in her wheelchair, and takes her with him wherever he goes. He does all this without complaining, without resentment. It is as natural for him as breathing.

Why? Because Bud is a man of character. He knows what matters in life and has intentionally focused on it all his days. He values his relationships with his wife and children. He has worked to provide what is necessary for their well-being, far beyond his own desires or pleasure. It never occurred to him to have an affair, get drunk, or desert his family. Bud has never let life's everyday discouragements, or even the tragedies that come his way, divert him from his goal of being a faithful person.

DOES CHARACTER COUNT?

One thing that Bud's story—and especially the last decade—should teach us as a nation is that character counts. As we are writing this book, Timothy McVeigh, the Oklahoma City bomber, waits for his execution. Outwardly he looks like the rest of us, but inside, character is absent, as evidenced by his lack of respect for human life.

Does a person's character make a difference in the way he lives, in the decisions he makes? Aren't values and morals just relative anyway, and at best, too personal to be important in one's public life? Does it really matter what one believes, what values he holds? Timothy McVeigh is one solid confirmation that character counts.

A widespread philosophy today declares that there is no absolute truth. Truth is only what one perceives at the moment. What feels true today may not feel true tomorrow. Note the use of the word *feel*. According to this view, the highest value is whatever one's emotions dictate. What is true for me today may or may not be true for me tomorrow based on how I feel. I may sincerely feel love for you today, but tomorrow, when the feeling has evaporated, my profession of love no longer is true, so I am not obligated to you in any way. My highest value is myself and my perception. No longer do I commit in marriage "until death do us part," but I promise to be faithful "for as long as love shall last."

Meg has been a clinician since 1979. And since Steve started New Life Clinics in 1988, New Life has become the largest provider of Christian treatment. Now he does a daily live call-in show that focuses on people and their emotional problems. Take it from two people who have dealt with people and their feelings for decades: feelings are a pretty crummy standard on which to base a life or a decision. Here is a piece of earth-shattering truth that we have learned. Your feelings have a point. But they are not the point. They have value but are not the most valuable criteria for decision making. Getting in touch with feelings should not mean detaching from what is true and right.

Some young people have become so disengaged from absolute truth and their personal responsibility that they seem to have no conscience at all. One young man, Dale, is sixteen years old, and an example of a disengagement from truth. His parents are also an example of the same, which makes it clear why the boy is so disengaged. Dale is eager to get his driving license. His parents have been taking him out for driving experience. They have become deeply concerned about his attitude. Typical interactions sound like these:

> "Son, try not to stop so abruptly. The cars behind you need warning so as to not hit you."
>
> "So what? It would be their fault if they hit me anyway."

Sure the boy is out of touch, but if you were a parent I would hope you would stop the car, get in the driver's seat, and resume drivers ed. in a year or two when the kid has some concept of responsibility.

> "Son, you need to observe ahead of time where the arrows are for the turn lanes. We needed to go straight, and now we are in the left-turn-only lane."
> "So? I will go straight anyway. They will just have to get out of my way."

Now that would have done it for me, but it did not register with Dale's parents. They had noticed a rather callous attitude before, but had attributed it to immaturity. They assumed he was just being a typically self-centered teenager. After these driving incidents, however, they began to recall other disturbing signs. A few months before, Dale had been dismissed from his job at a local electronics store because he had stolen a pair of headphones. (That act alone would have prevented me from even considering his getting a driver's license.) He had taken them home and used them for four days before the manager figured out what had happened. When confronted, Dale denied stealing and said he had just "forgotten to pay for them." He thought it very unfair that he was fired. Sadly his parents believed him.

At his next job he was insulted when the boss tried to tell him how to dress professionally and thought it was "picky" that his supervisor wrote him up for being late three days in a row. Dale repeatedly rearranged his schedule behind the supervisor's back, and the supervisor did not discover Dale had switched with someone until the time of the shift. Dale complained to his parents about how stupid it was that the supervisor said he had to okay any future shift changes.

As Dale's mom began to put the pieces together, she recalled a recent interaction about a jacket he had purchased, worn three or four times, and then announced he was returning to the store. She said, "Son, you cannot return that. You have already worn it. That is not honest." His response was, "So? I will just rip out the zipper and tell them it was defective. No one will know or care."

As Dale and his parents illustrate, our society is one that questions the very idea of values, morality, or absolutes. Fifty years ago there was a consensus in our country, and indeed the Western world in general, that the Judeo-Christian worldview should shape our behaviors. Even those who were not religious assented to the common values characterized by the Ten Commandments. Postmodern thinkers today question the idea of any one group suggesting that its way is absolute. Everything has become radically relative. But it is not. Truth is truth.

The Bible offers a reality based on truth; not mere intellectual information, feelings, or philosophy, but truth derived from an authentic experience with God. What changed the disciples from a bunch of mealymouthed cowards hiding in the upper room to men and women who changed the world? Surely not a new philosophy or a new religious system. The world was (and is) full of those. What radicalized their lives was encountering the risen Jesus. I have always been impressed that these faithful men and women became willing to die for Jesus. After His ascension, they did not give up, they pressed forward with new motivation. And the world was never the same.

Character really does count. And it comes as a result of absorbing and practicing wisdom and truth and making decisions that reflect them. Truth and wisdom do not come from people, they come from God. And in relationship with God, we have power to live the life we want, man or no man in the picture. The apostle Paul was eager that Christ's followers' faith "might not rest on men's wisdom, but on God's power" (1 Cor. 2:5). Be sure that you date someone who is more focused on the truth that comes from God, as spelled out in His Word, than the weird foolishness that pops up in the minds of people.

You need to start with, and stick to, a standard. Do you want a man who does what is right in his own eyes with no regard for spiritual truth? Does it matter? You bet it does. Ask any woman who has just found out that her husband of twelve or twenty or thirty years is entrapped in the snare of pornography and uses the excuse, "Everyone does it." Ask any young person suffering from a sexually transmitted disease. Ask the child whose mom, to feed her crack-cocaine habit, leaves her alone all day. But more important, ask *yourself* if you really want to spend your life with a man full of ego and pride and void of conscience.

It is true that not all unsaved people lack conscience. In fact, many of them live moral lives. But their character is based on something less sturdy than God's truth. Their commitment to strong values may vary from yours if you lead a biblically based life.

The bottom line is, God gives us the freedom to choose whom we date and whom we marry. We have to decide how we are going to make that decision, and this is reflected in how we live our lives: our way or God's way. It is our choice. We can choose spouses who show strong, God-based character, or we can suffer the consequences.

A MAN OF FAITH

Okay, so you find a man with character, a man whose values match yours. If you meet a guy who says all the right things—that he wants to do things God's way—how do you tell if he is for real? How do you know he is not just putting on an act to win you over? How do you know if he is sincere in his faith?

Many times we have counseled individuals who were scammed in this regard. That is, they thought their intended was a sincere person who trusted God, only to find out after the wedding that it was not true. Just as in wartime, today we see many "foxhole conversions": when it comes to winning the one they love, many men are less than honest about their true spiritual commitment. The Christian woman thinks, *God hasn't brought me a stellar Christian guy, so I guess I'll just have to trust that So-and-So will grow. Surely God would not want me to be alone, or at least not to wait any longer. So-and-So is open to spiritual things, and I do love him.* So she accepts whatever affirmations the beloved is willing to give, and hopes for the best.

How do you know if a person's faith is real? By looking at the results of his faith in his life. What spiritual fruit is the man producing on a regular basis? Jesus said that we will know the faithful by their actions or fruit (Luke 6:43–45). What fruit are we looking for? Paul answered this very clearly in his letter to the Christians in Galatia:

> You . . . were called to be free. But do not use your freedom to indulge the sinful nature; rather, serve one another in love. The entire law is summed up in a single command: "Love your neighbor as yourself." If you keep on biting and devouring each other, watch out or you will be destroyed by each other.
>
> So I say, live by the Spirit, and you will not gratify the desires of the sinful nature. . . .
>
> The acts of the sinful nature are obvious: sexual immorality, impurity and debauchery; idolatry and witchcraft; hatred, discord, jealousy, fits of rage, selfish ambition, dissensions, factions and envy; drunkenness, orgies, and the like. I warn you . . . that those who live like this will not inherit the kingdom of God.
>
> But the fruit of the Spirit is love, joy, peace, patience, kindness, goodness, faithfulness, gentleness and self-control. . . . Those who belong to Christ Jesus have crucified the sinful nature with its pas-

sions and desires. Since we live by the Spirit, let us keep in step with the Spirit. Let us not become conceited, provoking and envying each other. (Gal. 5:13–16, 19–26)

Let's examine this passage. How do we know if someone is truly a man of faith? He puts his life under the guidance of the Holy Spirit and produces the fruit of the Holy Spirit. So ask yourself: What fruit is your man consistently producing? Is he full of love, joy, peace, patience, kindness, goodness, and faithfulness? Or is he selfishly ambitious, causing disagreements everywhere he goes? Is he a peacemaker or a quarreller? Is he known for taking sides, and stirring up hatred and discord? Or is he peaceable, gentle, and self-disciplined? Is he a carouser, a drunk, or a sexual predator? Does he excuse immorality, impurity, or debauchery (leading others astray morally)? A person who is truly a man or woman of faith, while not perfect by any means (Rom. 7), has a reliable pattern in his or her life that bears the fruit of the Holy Spirit.

Some people talk a good line but do not live it out. Obviously, you have to know someone for a good length of time to see his character in many different venues. Anyone can look good for three months! Let others who know you well get to know him well too. While there are con artists who fool us, usually those close to us have a pretty good ability to smell a phony.

One final note on faith: We often are asked what a woman should do if she is involved with a man who does not believe the way she does. This is tough because there are many wonderful men who do not believe. But when you date someone who does not, you show that person how little a priority faith is in your life. You may say it is number one, but your acceptance shows him otherwise.

But when a woman says to a man, "I can't date you because I cannot share with you the most important part of my life," it has an impact. Life is too short to live it with a person without character and without faith.

A MAN OF PURPOSE

Purpose is a very important yet subtle quality. Mr. Right is going to be a man of purpose, a man with the ability to have and to set a direction in life. He is a man who knows his goal, his calling in life. Some men have obsessive priorities. Some have no priorities at all. Both reveal a lack of purpose. And some men know what God has designed them to do and be.

A man of purpose knows who he is, where he is from, and where he is going. Jesus was such a person. It is no wonder that all of history was changed as a result of Jesus' short visit to our planet. Look at who this Man was. The gospel of John records that Jesus knew He came from the Father, and was going back to the Father, and that He had all authority from the Father (John 13:3). He knew what He was to accomplish and when He had accomplished it (John 17:4). He knew that His task was to seek and to save the ones who were lost (Luke 19:10); to open the eyes of the blind, to preach the good news to the poor, and to proclaim freedom to the prisoners (Luke 4:18–19). He did not judge His success by the number of followers who came after Him. He did not look to others for approval. He just knew what He was supposed to do, and He did it.

Some people have no purpose. Or their purpose changes with the company they keep. Many today have no guiding principle, no rudder to steer by. So they drift aimlessly in the sea of life, often heading blindly for shipwreck. The Bible says such a person "is a double-minded man, unstable in all he does" (James 1:8).

God does not ridicule us if we need wisdom, but encourages us to seek it from Him (James 1:5; Prov. 2:1–6). A man of purpose knows when to ask for help. He knows that his purpose in life is bigger than himself and his own gratification. He is able to see beyond his nose. Seeking the noble and the uplifting, he is not willing to settle for small-minded pleasures. Yet he is not obsessed or controlled in a sick way by his purpose, the way a workaholic or a demagogue is. Instead he is shaped by it and molds his behavior in tune with its demands.

Let us suggest a first step when it comes to purpose and men. Don't look for a man until you have found *your* purpose. Then find a man who can help you live out *your* God-given purpose. What kind of purpose do *you* have? What purpose do you want the father of your children to have? What matters in your life? What will make you proud on your fiftieth wedding anniversary? What goals are you striving for now? What is your God-given calling?

Sometimes we settle too easily when we ought to reach higher. Do not settle for any man who pays attention to you. Strive to be a person of purpose and principle yourself, and you will find yourself attracted, and attractive, to Mr. Right, a man of purpose.

When it comes to character, faith, and purpose, many women miss the mark. They look for a man, and then let his character, faith, and purpose define theirs. We challenge that. First develop your faith. First set your values and live by them. First find the purpose for which God created you. If that purpose is to stay home and raise great kids, find a man who loves kids and desires a wife who stays at home and raises them. If your purpose is to do cancer research, be sure the man you are looking for appreciates the brilliance of a researcher and knows that much of your life will be spent in the lab and in the library. Identify yourself, then identify the man you are looking for.

CHAPTER 6

A MAN OF SELF-CONTROL
AND SOUND THINKING

Have you ever met a control freak? You know, someone who has to know where you are at every moment of the day. Someone who is always doubting you, always questioning and always intimidating you so they can be in control. Some control freaks are perfectionists and only feel in control when everything around them is in proper order. Some are anything but perfectionists, and they want control because they want their sloppy world to stay just as it is. Either version of a control freak makes everyone miserable with his controlling behavior and rigid, unsound thinking.

WHAT SELF-CONTROL IS—AND IS NOT

Some people like to control things. Others enjoy controlling people. Some have delusions of grandeur and try to control everything and everybody. They seem intent even on mastering ultimate self-control. Every hair is in place, every speck of dandruff banished, every syllable precise, every cough discreet. If they cannot win you with charm, they use bullying and manipulation. Control is their game, and they play it well. And they always act cool and collected.

Yet somehow they seem wound up tighter than a spring in Big Ben. You look at them and wonder if they will just explode (or maybe implode) some day. They almost seem to be "white-knuckling" through life, as if by sheer willpower they can make the world conform to their wishes.

Is this the type of self-discipline we think Mr. Right should have? No, no, no! What control freaks exhibit is *over*control, not self-control. True self-control involves mastery of one's self, one's passions, one's egocentrism, one's lust for attention, power, and dominance. It takes skill and diligence to become self-controlled.

Anyone who has been around babies knows that they do not have the ability to master themselves and their passions. They cannot control their bowels, much less their emotions! Fine muscle control is almost nonexistent for infants. They cannot use a spoon or drink from a cup. This is not because they are innately stupid, but because they have not yet matured enough to develop the necessary musculature. They are still babes, still maturing, still growing. They are learning to control their mouths and the sounds that come out of them. They are learning to crawl, stumble, fall, and walk.

No one expects a toddler to have the same degree of self-control as an adolescent. Why? Because we recognize that people develop into what they become as adults. Society is rather unforgiving toward those who will not mature. No one has much sympathy for the person who insists on talking gibberish when he or she is capable of speaking sense like an adult. No one with any sense tolerates a perfectly capable "child" of eighteen or older who refuses to work or go to school.

As people mature they are more able to understand the concepts of law or the Ten Commandments or doing something for "the common good" as opposed to self-interest. In the higher stages of moral development, a person becomes able to set aside self and mere physical pleasures, and choose the noble, the great, the triumphant for its own sake.

Unfortunately, many folks get stuck at a primitive level of maturity, the one that makes them decide issues based on what they can get out of them. We call it the "I'll scratch your back, you scratch mine" level. While many people can and some do rise above this immature level, a vast majority cannot be bothered. Why? Because it would involve self-control, discipline, and sound thinking. And those things are too much work. It might cost them something.

How mature are you? And if you are dating someone, how mature is he?

THE BENEFITS OF
SELF-CONTROL/SOUND THINKING

Controlling oneself for the common good or for the good of one's future, one's children, one's country, or one's God has gone quite out of fashion. With the sixties came the "let it all hang out" philosophy, along with "Whatever feels good, do it." Freedom was celebrated, if not worshiped: freedom from controls, freedom from bondage to the "establishment," freedom from guilt, shame, and remorse. Today, we find a similar idea floating around in our world: *Do only what works for you, regardless of how it affects other people. Self-control is a rigid, antiquated concept. Be yourself and let everyone else adapt.*

The fact is, self-control is one of those traits that we need to live the life we want. And the man you marry needs to have self-control also. It is one of the priorities the Bible recommends for successful living. The apostle Paul wrote letters to a young man named Timothy, whom he had trained in spiritual things. Paul could see that Timothy had a bundle of potential, but the youth feared maturity and life's temptations. So Paul wrote these thoughts to him:

> I remind you to fan into flame the gift of God, which is in you . . . For God did not give us a spirit of timidity, but a spirit of power, of love and of self-discipline. (2 Tim. 1:6–7)

> Endure hardship with us like a good soldier of Christ Jesus. No one serving as a soldier gets involved in civilian affairs—he wants to please his commanding officer. Similarly, if anyone competes as an athlete, he does not receive the victor's crown unless he competes according to the rules. (2 Tim. 2:3–5)

> Flee the evil desires of youth, and pursue righteousness, faith, love and peace, along with those who call on the Lord out of a pure heart. (2 Tim. 2:22)

Paul was urging Timothy to be a man of self-control! Another term for self-control could be *sound judgment*. Paul told Timothy to avoid "godless chatter" so he could become more and more godly. He reminded him to avoid "foolish and stupid arguments" because they produced quarrels (2 Tim. 2:16, 23). He wanted Timothy to be sober- and clear-minded. And this would require self-control.

In short, Paul wanted Timothy to be a Mr. Right! He longed to see Timothy mature into a man who was able to discipline himself for godly behavior. Mr. Right is a person who knows how to let the Lord work in him to achieve the self-control and sound thinking that are the fruit of God's Spirit, not his own efforts. Paul knew that as Timothy cooperated with the work of God's Spirit within him, he would find himself doing the things that please God rather than having to "white-knuckle" his way through life.

Mr. Right is a man who understands this process and while not perfect, he is self-controlled, sober-minded, able to think and act soundly in most situations. He is not a control freak, nor is he codependent or wishy-washy.

How can you tell if your Mr. Right is a man of discipline and sound thinking? Consider the following questions:

- Is he consistent in lifestyle habits such as grooming, eating, sleeping, cleaning his apartment, paying bills, and so on?

- Does he struggle with excess in some area, such as spending, drugs, alcohol, eating, gambling, video games, fast driving, sexual activity?

- Is he able to control his temper even if under pressure? Or if he is provoked, do even small issues set him off?

- Is he careful in his speech and what he says in front of those who might be offended or hurt by his words?

- Does he manage his health wisely by eating right, exercising, and taking medicine as prescribed?

- Is he consistent in his relationships? Is he the same with you in public as in private? Is he the same at church as at work or school?

- Does he have control of his emotions, or does he let his moods dominate?

- Is he careful to say no when it is appropriate and to set limits with others who may try to take advantage of him?

- Does he know his own limitations and weaknesses well enough that he can protect himself from sin when he is vulnerable?

- Can he say no to you in the appropriate situations?

A man who is able to discipline himself without being a control freak is a real gem. Just as precious is a man who, trained by God's Spirit and God's Word, can think clearly and rationally. You are fortunate if you find him.

CHAPTER 7

A MAN OF LOVE, LAUGHTER, AND LEARNING

The right man is always a unique combination of many characteristics, strengths, and weaknesses. You have to take the whole package, the good and the bad. And there will be some bad. By bad we mean things that will irritate and annoy you. The very things that were so attractive to you at one point may be sources of difficulty later. How do you deal with these realities? Everyone handles them differently, but there is one thing that will help everyone. When Mr. Right is a man who loves, laughs, and learns through life, it makes the unbearable much more bearable. It enables you to move beyond the irritations to a deepening connection. These traits are so valuable in a man, and they seem to be the commonalities that help a good relationship grow even in the midst of some painful life events that are bound to come along, sooner or later.

A MAN OF LOVE

Of course you want a man of love. But what does he look like? Answers differ. A recent article described how the image of what is attractive to a woman nowadays has changed from fifty years ago. No longer the strong, silent type, the new-millennium Mr. Right is supposedly all sensitivity and compliments: empathic and caring, kind and warm, eager to talk and share his feelings. It is a whole new world. Once a woman felt loved if her husband came home for dinner. Today he had better come home, tell her dinner was great, *and* help with the dishes.

Do not misunderstand: we are not eager to return to the past. We just want to point out that how we define a loving person can depend upon our ages, our culture, or our expectations.

So where can we turn for a timeless description of a loving man? First Corinthians 13 in the New Testament. This chapter is read more at weddings than any other. Even non-churchgoers are familiar with at least parts of it. Songs have been inspired by its prose. Sermons have been preached. What is the point? In verses 1–3 Paul, the author, points out that even if you are the most talented person in your group, the most amazing orator, or the best visionary, without love all of your activities are pointless. Then he defines truly meaningful and godly behavior:

> Love is patient, love is kind. It does not envy, it does not boast, it is not proud. It is not rude, it is not self-seeking, it is not easily angered, it keeps no record of wrongs. Love does not delight in evil but rejoices with the truth. It always protects, always trusts, always hopes, always perseveres.
>
> Love never fails. (1 Cor. 13:4–8)

According to God's Word, if Mr. Right is a man of love, what characteristics will he exhibit?

LOVE IS PATIENT, LOVE IS KIND

Do you know someone who is patient? Meg's brother-in-law, Andrew Briggs, is an extremely patient man. Maybe you have to be patient to learn to take a small airplane apart and put it back together again by yourself; or to build an airstrip in the jungle without the aid of modern earth-moving machines; or to fly mile after mile over vast jungles with nothing to guide you but your instruments, instinct, and an old map. There are no satellite guidance systems for a Missionary Aviation Fellowship pilot. Andy is a gem.

Andy's strength is based on his deep love for Jesus Christ and his submission to Him in every area of life. His wife and five kids will assure you that he is not perfect, but they will also affirm his kindness and patience. He is a safe, trustworthy person to be around, and his family knows it. They can turn to him in any circumstance, secure in the knowledge that he won't bite their heads off with impatient remarks or nonverbal responses that push them away. He is a man of love. If you are going to be with a man, that is the kind of man you need.

LOVE DOES NOT ENVY, BOAST, OR SEEK ATTENTION

Love is not jealous, over-competitive, seeking to win at all costs. Love is happy when others succeed. Love does not need to promote self. Do you know anyone like this?

Arnold was an assistant administrator at a local hospital. One of the things Arnold learned early in life was how to play second fiddle without resentment. The hospital where he served was known all over the world for its high quality of care. Located in a prestigious part of a large metropolitan area, it was known as state-of-the-art. Many came to see it and learn from Arnold's boss, who was held in highest esteem in the medical profession. "Quality care from happy doctors" was his motto. Thus he was sought after, honored, and celebrated on a regular basis.

Those second in command rarely get as much of the limelight as number one, if any. Arnold spoke publicly occasionally, but most of his work took place behind the scenes. Arnold took all this in stride.

He was talented, educated, and loved his boss, and he was content to fulfill his own role without a hint of jealousy or envy; without any bitterness or need to point out his talents or successes. Arnold never sought first place, but as John the Baptist did for Jesus, he sought to make his boss successful. Consequently, he will never be forgotten by the many people whose lives he has touched. Those people are not the ones who came to be healed, but the ones who worked for that healing. While they loved the vision of his boss, they loved the heart of Arnold who was always looking after their needs. When he died, the church could not contain the entire crowd.

LOVE IS NOT RUDE, IT IS NOT EASILY ANGERED

Some people can cut you to ribbons with one word. Some are so irritable you'd think they slept all night with a rattlesnake. Mr. Right has a grip on his tongue. He lets others speak, and listens when they do. He may have a definite opinion and probably can articulate it, but he is not apt to fly off the handle if you disagree with him. He is not prone to using sarcasm to make his point.

Our friend Glen is a great example of this. Glen, though he admits to "losing it" once in a while, is someone who would find it difficult to be rude, crude, or easily provoked. Glen has worked with people of many different beliefs and backgrounds, yet he has never acted as if this mattered at all. Over the last twenty-five years he has been placed in many difficult situations. Yet Glen has a gift for being able to say the right, kind, helpful thing at the right moment. He seeks to see the best even in those who have hurt him or been rude to him. He, too, is a man of love.

LOVE KEEPS NO RECORD OF WRONGS AND REJOICES IN TRUTH

How many of us can say we don't have a list of slights, hurts, or sins others have committed against us? How many of us can genuinely rejoice in the truth, rather than gloat when the truth comes out? Mr. Right is a man who does not need to bring up every little mistake you ever made to prove he is right. He is eager for others to shine. He wants the truth even if it is painful. He is not afraid of the truth. Even when someone has wronged him, he is not willing to easily give up on him. He is not eager to see wickedness punished but longs for grace even for the ones who do wrong.

Love Always Protects, Hopes, Trusts, and Perseveres

A man of love perseveres when life gets tough. Mr. Right knows how to see beyond the moment. He is able to love because God has loved him. He has received grace for his own failures and weaknesses, so he can extend it hopefully and trustingly to others. He seeks to protect others and their reputations. He would never make mother-in-law jokes or ridicule someone's friends or family.

A man of love is like Jesus. He accepts people where they are but challenges them to grow, hopes they will, and cheers them on when they struggle.

Love Never Fails

All people fail, but love never does. What does this mean for Mr. Right? Mr. Right may mess up, but he knows he is still loved by the One who never fails. Therefore he is not overcome by his human mistakes. He puts his faith in the God who is love itself—the One who created love. Love never fails because when it is true love it cannot fail. It is not based on looks or mood, it is based on a commitment of undying dedication and devotion. If people would only follow the vows they made to love through the best and worst all the way to the end, the world would see love in action during illnesses, mental breakdowns, job losses, and disappointments. But because the world does not really understand love, sometimes it never experiences it in its richest form. That variety of love is always coming back for more, always persevering, always loving.

A MAN OF LAUGHTER

Mr. Right is not a jokester or a clown, but a man who knows how to respond to life with humor—with deep, belly-aching, uproarious, outrageous laughter. With silly, tickle-you-in-bed laughter. With hide-and-seek, breakfast-in-bed laughter. He finds the absurdity and chuckles in broken water pipes in the basement, in the flat tire, in the tenth dirty diaper of the day, in sex, in the rain during a camp out.

Some people say to be wary of a man who cannot cry. Perhaps we should say the same about a man who cannot laugh. A man who laughs is able to laugh at himself. He can take a joke, not just tease or pull pranks on others. He can laugh at the antics of children and animals with equal pleasure. He is not necessarily sophisticated or even witty. He just knows not to take life (or himself) too seriously.

Laughter is good medicine, the Bible says. And actually, modern medical research confirms this ancient idea. People who laugh live longer. They are sick less, and when they do get sick they recover faster. So much of life is hard that we all need to seek out opportunities to kick back and laugh.

Mr. Right is going to know how and when to laugh. He will not necessarily be extroverted or the life of the party, but he will know how to chuckle, chortle, and guffaw. His eyes will sometimes have a twinkle and he might wink to show his pleasure and joy. He will want to include you in his laughter. He may be quiet, but at times he can be hilarious. He knows how to have fun, and how to encourage others with laughter. Nothing makes for a happier home than parents who know how to laugh. Be sure your Mr. Right is one of those.

There are some fundamental elements that make a marriage work and then endure when it does not work so well. At the top of that list, right behind faith, is a sense of humor. The couples who stay together, even through the tough stuff, have a common language of humor. They have little inside jokes that they can communicate with a quick glance. They have the ability to look back on the past and laugh at what once made them cry. Be sure that when your Mr. Right packs a suitcase for the honeymoon, he lays laughter right on top. It will help the rest of what he packs from getting too wrinkled.

A MAN OF LEARNING

Does this mean your Mr. Right has to have a college degree? While that would not hurt, it is by no means a necessity. We are not focusing on scholarship as much as openness.

We've all met someone who thought he knew it all. Know-it-alls are not much fun to be around, are they? Some people just have to be right, even when they are wrong! You can hear it coming—you tell a story about your kids, your family, or your church, and they reply, "I can top that!" Their children never get tired, never fuss over what to eat, never sass. Know-it-alls keep house perfectly and the garbage disposal never backs up on them. Their pets are perfectly, trained. They know every remedy for every malady and are not afraid to tell you about them. If you seem less than receptive, they just repeat themselves *ad nauseam*. They often preface their remarks with, "I know it is none of my business, but . . ." or "You know, it would really be better if you would just . . ."

What makes know-it-alls tick? Why are they so defensive of their own ways and so closed to other people's ideas or feelings? Sometimes it is insecurity. Somewhere, somehow, they concluded, *It's not okay to be wrong, so I had better always be right.* So even though they feel unsure, they act as if they know it all. They are afraid that you might be right, and then they are sure the world will fall in (at least metaphorically), and so they protest that they are right even in face of evidence to the contrary.

For some, though, pride is a know-it-all's passion. He really is convinced that he is the master of the universe. Even God ought to ask his opinion. He knows the right way to do, to think, to feel, and heaven forbid you would ever disagree.

Mr. Right, on the other hand, is a man who has a teachable spirit. He has a humble heart and is able to take criticism and constructive feedback without defensiveness. He does not have to check a person's credentials or education, age, gender, or economic status in order to be willing to learn from him or her. Mr. Right does not look at the world through egotistical or egocentric glasses. He realizes that others have a perspective that is needed to balance his own. He may firmly hang on to his beliefs, but he can also genuinely listen to and understand an opposing view.

The desire to learn is one of those character issues that must not be ignored. Those who are encased in their own perspective from their own experiences are not only blind, they are very difficult to love through the years. Look for a man who enjoys getting out of himself and his predictable world to learn through experience as well as being taught. And be sure Mr. Right is a man who respects women, especially you, and believes he can learn much from women, especially you. If not, your strengths will never compensate for his weaknesses and your weaknesses will be held against you rather than understood. And if he is a real learner, the thing he will want to learn most is you.

Is the relationship all about him, or do you have a place? That is a major clue as to whether or not he has a desire to learn. And Mr. Right is always a learner.

MATTERS OF A MAN'S HEART

Often women focus on the wrong traits and mistake character flaws for strengths. They desire the confident, self-assured man, and mistakenly end up with an uncaring and demanding jerk. Wanting strength, they may shun a man who has a sensitive side, who actually is interested in who they are and how to please them.

The heart of a man is the most important part of his anatomy. While the world looks at the exterior, the wise woman looks for the inner man who is secure enough to love, free enough to laugh, and humble enough to learn. If you don't focus on the inside of a man, you may end up with someone who focuses only on your exterior as well. If so, when the years wash away some physical beauty, the tide will take out your relationship too.

You deserve a man who is able to see the giftedness in others and not be threatened by it; a man whose love is ignited by joy rather than lust, charity rather than greed, opportunity rather than desperation. He can learn from the janitor in the plant or the scholar at the university. His faith expands because of his strong desire for God and his efforts to learn more about God.

Mr. Right loves, laughs, and learns because it is God's design for him. He understands the role God has assigned him and his mate. He knows that God created woman to be a companion who fits in with him in just the right way—"bone of [his] bones and flesh of [his] flesh" (Gen. 2:23). He recognizes with Adam, the first man, the complementary nature of the two sexes imaging the nature of God Himself (Gen. 1:26–27). He knows that a woman is God's unique creation and appreciates her gifts, strengths, and talents. He knows that she is valued as much by God as he is.

A man of love, laughter, and learning: that is Mr. Right, and he is looking for a Ms. Right who is of the same substance.

CHAPTER 8

TEN WARNING SIGNS MR. RIGHT MAY ACTUALLY BE MR. WRONG

In our first book, *Avoiding Mr. Wrong,* we listed numerous ways women could identify a bad guy masquerading as a good one, and make wise decisions if she was dating or married to him. While many women compose lists of qualities they want in a guy, it is equally important to know what you are *not* looking for and why you are attracted to the very person that may cause you a lifetime of pain. Our purpose here is to summarize some of the most significant qualities of Mr. Wrong so you can steer clear of this guy.

If you want more information about Mr. Wrong, you can find it in our book *Avoiding Mr. Wrong (And What to Do if You Didn't): Ten Men Who Will Ruin Your Life* (Thomas Nelson Publishers, 2000).

Remember: Some Mr. Wrongs will have only one of the traits we list—some may have all ten. Read these carefully and see if you are attached or attracted to one of these dangerous men.

TEN CLUES THAT MR. WRONG IS NEAR

1. MR. WRONG LOOKS FOR EASY TARGETS

Easy targets include weak women who have low self-esteem and a desperate need to take care of someone; women who are afraid to be alone; women who are newly divorced or widowed. Mr. Wrong doesn't want you to notice that your attraction to him is really avoidance of something else, such as loneliness.

2. MR. WRONG WANTS EVERYTHING NOW

This includes your full, undivided attention, your adoration, your body. He rushes talk of marriage, pushes for sex early in the relationship, disrespects your boundaries, demonstrates little ability for delayed gratification, fears emotional intimacy, and emphasizes the physical.

3. MR. WRONG HIDES THINGS

He may hide information, personal issues, financial problems, weaknesses, emotions. It may not be what he says that creates conflict, but what he leaves unsaid. The classic example is the man who "forgets" to tell you he is already married or "separated, but not quite divorced." He can't seem to tell the truth no matter what, and you often feel in your gut that he is deceiving you. He insists that "white lies" do not count and that it is okay to lie "if you do not get caught." He tends to leave out parts of the truth that later turn out to be pivotal.

4. MR. WRONG LOOKS BAD TO YOUR LOVED ONES

If your friends and family have serious doubts about the guy you are dating, do not let your hunger for a relationship blind you to the real character of your man. Loved ones can often spot things about a man that you are not able to see clearly at first. Do not discount negative feedback from people who know you.

5. Mr. Wrong Has a Hot Temper

He flares up about insignificant things. He may or may not be physically violent. He is often inordinately jealous and always insists that he is clearly right, even if the facts are against him. He may be charming one minute and then raging the next. You find yourself confused and wondering what *you* did to cause him to change so dramatically. You walk on eggshells, not wanting to incite him accidentally.

6. Mr. Wrong Can Be Picky

He can also be controlling and rigid. You find him much more than fastidious: he is fanatical. He adjusts picture frames in public waiting rooms, gets angry if his car gets crumbs in it, and picks the lint off of your coat. He constantly finds fault in your housekeeping. Or he can be the opposite: obsessively messy. He calls it "creative," but your mom would say he is a slob.

7. Mr. Wrong May Be Looking for a Mom

With this type of Mr. Wrong, you end up feeling as if you have adopted a child instead of married an adult. He can be quite the genius about things that intrigue him but, like a young child, is pretty helpless when it suits his purpose. He lets you do the hard emotional work for the relationship and seems to come alive only when fun is involved.

8. Mr. Wrong Can Seem Too Good to Be True

That is because he is. At first you think he is wonderful, and you marvel at his ability to charm the fuzz off a peach. Sooner or later, though, you realize that he uses his gift of gab to talk himself out of any responsibility or blame. You notice that he often acts as if the rules do not apply to him, and he expects you and everyone else to make exceptions for him.

9. MR. WRONG CAN BE TOO FAITHLESS OR TOO RELIGIOUS

He may be indifferent to faith and values, or obsessed with them. He can be an atheist or a churchgoer, but in either case he carries an anger about his devotion. He may be a cowardly person who is afraid to set boundaries or to take a stand, or he may be an obnoxious crusader ready to change you into what he thinks you ought to be.

10. MR. WRONG MIGHT BE UNCARING

He sometimes is indifferent toward or uninterested in you or other people, despite their pleas for attention. This type of Mr. Wrong is a passive person who just seems to be along for the ride. You find that having meaningful conversations with him is like pulling teeth and getting him to follow through on commitments makes you suicidal. When you protest his lack of involvement, he insists that he loves you and will do anything to improve the relationship. But the changes are always short-lived, and you end up feeling even more angry.

RATE YOUR MAN

There are different degrees of wrongness. Some men have just one area that is a little worse than the rest. Others are in very bad shape. Now that you have an idea of what Mr. Wrong could look like, you can evaluate any guy you are dating to determine whether or not he will lead you to misery if you continue to be with him.

Answer the following questions. The more Yes answers, the more chance your Mr. Right is actually Mr. Wrong.

• Do your family and/or friends disapprove of the relationship?

- Does he treat his mom and/or sisters with disdain and disrespect?

- Has he been divorced more than once?

- Is he obsessed with religion or with avoiding it?

- Are you concerned about his use of alcohol, drugs, or other substances?

- Does he treat you with disrespect, contempt, or disdain?

- Has he ever been violent with you or others?

- Does he consistently put his needs ahead of yours or his children's?

- Do you suspect that more often than not, he is not telling you the truth?

- Does he show job instability?

- Do you feel that the relationship's success depends on you?

- Does he resent your relationships with friends, family, coworkers?

- Does he seem inordinately jealous?

- Does he lose his temper over small things?

- Does he sponge off of you or friends or family?

- Does he excuse his use of pornography or gambling?

- Would you be unhappy if your daughter married a man like him?

- Has he pressured you to go further sexually than you were ready for?

- Does he seem to resent your successes?

- Does he seem totally indifferent to your real needs, thoughts, and feelings?

If you make an honest assessment of the man you are with and he is not measuring up, you need to think of the pain it would cause to move on. But more importantly you need to think of the pain it would cause to *not* move on. Unfortunately, many Mr. Wrongs are not so obvious in their display of disorders. Sometimes it is difficult to notice that a man may be Mr. Wrong, because he is wearing a disguise. He seems to be one way but underneath is a different animal!

FAVORITE DISGUISES WORN BY MR. WRONG

If I wanted to buy a CD from you with a counterfeit twenty-dollar bill, if I had any sense at all I would not attempt to hand you a pink, purple, or yellow piece of paper. I would do well in my deception to hand you a bill with the same coloring as real currency has.

The same applies with Mr. Wrong. The worst men are not going to look like axe murderers. In fact, Mr. Wrong may disguise himself as the nicest, most wonderful man you could ever imagine. Here are some common disguises worn by many Mr. Wrongs.

1. MR. MONEYBAGS

Just because a man is a millionaire does not mean he is Mr. Right. He may have money but no character.

2. MR. SUPERSUCCESS

Being financially successful does not equal being Mr. Right. (Being a failure doesn't either!) Successful is as successful does. What kind of success do you value in the long run? Are only the men who are at the top of their fields worth the title of Mr. Right? No way. A man may be a success in his career and a real dud in relationships.

3. MR. STATUS SYMBOL

Once more: prestige is nice, but it is not a guarantee that a man is a good man for you. Even Princess Grace of Monaco and certainly Princess Diana found out that marrying a prince is not all it is cracked up to be.

4. MR. WONDERFUL (ALIAS MR. PERFECT)

Remember, if something seems too good to be true, it probably is. Especially if he is the one who tells you how wonderful he is.

5. MR. SUPERSTAR

Whether he's a rock star, a sports hero, or movie big shot, the chances of his being your Mr. Right are quite small. Most of these types are more in love with themselves than they ever will be with anyone else.

6. MR. STUD (ALIAS MR. ROMANCE)

This guy brings roses on the first date, takes you to the opera, and sweeps you off your feet. He also gets your hormones racing, but that is about all he has in mind.

7. MR. TOO SENSITIVE

If this is the Mr. Wrong we think it is, he is actually Mr. "I Wonder if I Am Gay." Gay men are often attractive to women because they are more in touch with the feminine aspect of their personalities and can relate emotionally better than most straight men. If a man has doubts about his sexual identity, he certainly is not ready to be Mr. Right.

8. MR. FAITHFUL

This man looks good especially if you are a deeply spiritual person yourself. Many religious men are sincere and apt to be good Mr. Rights. However, some use religion as a psychological tool to manipulate others or to assuage inner guilt or pain. Some use their faith to bolster their misogynistic views or to justify abuse against women. While they may be in the minority, these men are out there.

9. MR. HUMBLE

This man has many good characteristics, but he cannot stand conflict and will avoid it at all costs. He may seem humble, but he is actually quite a coward. He will placate you, give in to you, and rarely reveal his true feelings out of fear of your possible anger. He is afraid of what you and others think. His sense of peace comes from a lack of conflict, not a deep, inner serenity.

10. MR. EMPATHY

This man is a good listener. He looks you in the eye, attends to your every word, and is always there to listen, comfort, and console. The problem is, he does not share his own feelings or thoughts very readily. You are the one who does the talking, and you cannot get him to divulge much about himself. He begins to seem more like your therapist than your boyfriend.

Once you are attracted to someone and have invested countless hours in the relationship, it is very hard to admit you have made a mistake, grieve your losses, and move on. But if you found the person you are dating described in this chapter, that is exactly what you need to do. Some of the most brilliant people in the world have married some of the sickest. A year of sadness is nothing compared to a lifetime of sadness.

It is no accident that you have found this book. What is the message that is meant for you? If it is to encourage you to evaluate your current relationship and the evaluation comes out pretty negative, then do the painful but right thing and move on. Mr. Right could be just around the corner, just over the hill, or just where you least expect him to be.

CHAPTER 9

WHAT MAKES MR. RIGHT MR. NOT RIGHT NOW

Sometimes you meet Mr. Right at the right time, in the right place, and the pieces come together smoothly. You are at the same level in your careers or education. You both have responsible jobs and can support yourselves. You have similar backgrounds and interests. Your families approve. In short, you have all your ducks in a row. So settling down and being committed seems like a good idea.

But something is not quite right. Perhaps the timing feels off or you sense a problem that does not make him Mr. Wrong, but causes you to wonder if you should wait. The fact is, sometimes Mr. Right is really Mr. Not Right Now. The ducks actually aren't "all in a row," or there are a few ducks missing. Whatever the case, it calls for you to duck away from a commitment until a few things are corrected. We have put together a list of ten types of men with whom you should wait to make a lifelong commitment. If any one of these begins to pressure you to marry, then he moves from the category of Mr. Not Right Now to Mr. Wrong.

ELEVEN CHARACTERISTICS OF
MR. NOT RIGHT NOW

1. MR. IMMATURITY

He has many good traits. He is similar to you in values, income, and background. He just needs to grow up. You notice that he is immature in a number of ways. For example, he is so insecure that he tries to control the relationship completely. He may seek power through material possessions, status, money, or influence. He has a hard time trusting anyone and tends to frame relationships in win-lose terms. You often feel as if you are in a power play even over stupid things.

Another pattern of immaturity you may run into is the self-deprecating habit. This man is always apologizing. He feels weak and never thinks he does things well enough. He has the idea in his head that other people must know better than he does. He tends to sacrifice his own needs to keep the relationship going, so as not to offend you.

Some immature people are intent on avoiding true connectedness with others. They may say that they want it, but either because they have never experienced a deep relationship, or because the close relationships they have had were filled with criticism and blame, they tend to keep others at arm's length. In that way, they cannot be hurt or have their expectations or hopes dashed. They are waiting for you to make the first move or to keep the relationship moving.

Maturity involves being able to make a successful adjustment to adult life. Mature people are aware of their own feelings and those of the people around them. They can handle emotionally charged situations in a reasonable, straightforward manner. They see themselves accurately and have a decent appreciation for their own motivations. They accept their strengths and weaknesses. They are able to plan for the future, make decisions, meet responsibilities, and do their share of the work. Generally, they are self-reliant, organized to some degree, and able to keep themselves and their environment neat and clean. Fair, honest, and sincere, if they are wrong, they can freely admit it and make amends.

The mature person has a degree of competence in maneuvering through the myriad of problems and circumstances that comes his way in life. Developing such competence takes hard work, patience, and the willingness to take up a challenge. Maturity also means having integrity or good character.

In order to have integrity, Mr. Right must show self-discipline and a commitment to ethical behavior. Integrity involves being congruent; as we have said, this means being consistently the same on the outside (in one's behavior) as on the inside (in one's heart or inner self). When we function congruently, we are closest to being our ideal selves. This integrity allows us to be trusted by others and, hence, capable of healthy relating.

Obviously, all of us are capable of maturing more and more as we grow older. Each day can be a new opportunity to grow in our level of emotional and ethical maturity. The question is: When are you mature enough to be in a committed, lifelong marriage relationship? Mr. Right is probably ready if he

- is able to accurately express and acknowledge his own and others' feelings.

- is curious, eager to learn.

- copes well with fears, anxieties, uncertainties, and mixed feelings.

- copes maturely with anger, frustration, discouragement, and rejection.

- is able to take responsibility for mistakes and failure.

- uses imagination creatively but is able to distinguish between reality and fantasy.

- accepts and approves of himself, and offers such acceptance to others.

- earns acceptance and approval from others in healthy ways.

- makes friends relatively easily, offering good treatment, affection, and consideration.

- keeps promises and follows through with projects.

- shares decision making and handles conflicts constructively.

- becomes more likeable by using feedback from others to grow and change.

- is able to share and is socially responsible.

- uses knowledge, skills, and abilities constructively and in pursuit of a goal.

- plans, takes initiative, and shows creativity.

- has realistic expectations of self and others.

- is self-reliant and able to take on challenges with a reasonable degree of caution.

- sets high standards for himself and is motivated to meet them.

- solves problems by being cooperative and flexible.

- develops a well-rounded life and has varied interests and activities.

- is patient, truthful, and able to delay gratification.

- uses self-control in dealing with unpleasantness and tries to be fair and constructive.

- is reasonably neat and reliable, able to respect the property rights and boundaries of other people.

If you are not finding many of these characteristics in your man, then do not rush into marriage. There are also some instances where you do not rush *out* of the relationship either. Consider the flaws that you see and determine whether or not with some time and maybe even some good counseling, he just might turn into Mr. Right. If so, and he is eager to grow and work on them, then there is still hope for the relationship. But when dealing with this type of man you must not listen to what he says or respond to his intentions, you must watch what he does. If he does nothing, move on.

2. Mr. Newly Separated, Divorced, or Widowed

No matter how bad or good a relationship was, there is always pain and a process of grief in letting go of it. That process takes time. We go through stages of grief. Because pain is uncomfortable, we may jump into another relationship to numb ourselves. While it may be okay to get a new puppy immediately when one's dog dies, it is not okay to get a new girlfriend or spouse immediately following the loss of human relationship. The longer the relationship lasted, the longer it will take to get over. If a man was married thirty years and then his spouse dies, he does not need another thirty years to recover, but he may need two or three years—at least.

Often we have seen people rebound into a relationship too quickly following a divorce or death. This rushing ahead can only make adjustment to being with someone new more difficult. Interestingly, many times, the rebounder picks someone uncannily like the person he lost, either in appearance, personality, or even name! Sometimes friends and family can see the resemblance, but the rebounder is totally unaware.

While no one can ever replace a loved one, we do learn to move on. We are able to appreciate the good from past relationships and learn from the bad. Time, however, is usually the mediator of such lessons.

When we do not give ourselves enough time to grieve, we are apt to just anesthetize the pain rather than truly engage in a new relationship. Waking up two or three years into a rebound relationship and realizing you were only reacting to your grief can have a devastating effect on a couple. All is not necessarily lost, but it can be very painful to all involved.

3. MR. ALL-TALK-AND-NO-ACTION

When a young woman comes to us for counseling and is so excited that she and "Johnny" are engaged, we always ask the defining question as to just what type of engagement it really is: "Do you have a ring and a date?" Until a guy is willing to make a commitment by putting his money where his mouth is, so to speak, forget it. If he is ready to move in but not ready to wed, he is *not ready* for anything. If he is willing to propose but is not in the financial position to buy a ring and provide a home, *wait*.

Why so many young women are willing to be "engaged" without a ring and a date is beyond us. If he is not mature enough to be able to do those two things, what makes you think he will be mature enough to stay married? Or that you will ever get married to him? Living together is a sign of immaturity, not wisdom. Only the mature are able to make a true marriage covenant. Mr. Right says

You are so important to me that I want to make this extraordinary commitment to you. I am willing to sacrifice myself and my possessions to provide a home for you and our children. I am done with childhood. I am ready to be a man. I am willing to take you on as my most intimate companion, come good or bad, easy or hard. I am finished looking around and have decided to be faithful in every way to you. I am glad to forsake all other female relationships in order to be exclusively wed to you. While my hormones and feelings may tempt me to do otherwise, I am willing to commit to you, and to you alone.

If he cannot say that, he is not ready. If you cannot say it, you are not ready. Do not think that a ring is enough. Too many women have ended up engaged for years and never wed. By the time they figure out he is all talk and no action, the old biological clock has been ticking, and she ends up getting desperate.

4. MR. EYEBALL

This man is not ready because he is still caught up in what the Bible calls the "lust of the eye." He likes to covet that which does not belong to him. He loves to ogle women. He notices, looks, and drives around the block to look again. He has a sore neck from all the turning around he does. He thinks pornography is okay for adults and that he "can handle it." He loves to "talk dirty" and to tell off-color jokes, even if you are embarrassed. He seems to regard his sexual member as his most important body part. He ridicules you for being such a "prude" or a "baby" when you complain about his voyeurism. He compares you subtly or overtly to women on TV, or in magazines or movies. He makes it clear you are not up to his sexual standard. He pushes you further than you feel comfortable going. He tries to run over your boundaries.

There is a small chance that this type of man may just be very immature, but there is a greater chance he may have a serious sexual addiction. It is difficult to tell at first. If he is just immature, then it will be a long time before he is ready for a relationship. Don't fall into the temptation to try to "grow him up." If you do, he will likely take you down with him. And if you have kids he could take them down with you also. So this man is to be avoided until he makes some major life changes that produce a growth in character, as unlikely as that might be.

If you are with someone who is claiming to be recovering from problems like these, be sure that the old behaviors are gone, not just underground, before you move the relationship along. Do not fall for the line or the assumption that he will not need the pornography once you are married, since he will have you. If he's addicted to it now, he will not get over it by being married to you. Also, be aware that where there is smoke (porn) there are probably one or two other sexually inappropriate habits as well. If you are naive on this subject you might read *Every Man's Battle* by Steve Arterburn, Fred Stoker, and Mike Yorkey, published by Waterbrook. The bigger issue is the lack of character and your attraction to such a man. Premarital counseling can often pick up on these types of issues and concerns. Treatment is available for pornography or sex addiction, and people can recover if they choose to do so. The support of a loving partner can be a help, but it is not the cure. Character is the cure, and character takes a long time to develop.

5. MR. DEBTOR

This fellow has a pile of debt and no reasonable plan to repay it. He may be in between jobs or just graduated from school and has not yet found his niche. If he expects you to work and put him through grad school, you may want to think about waiting until he is done (or get a good prenuptial agreement). Too many women have slaved away at low-paying jobs to put hubby through grad school, only to be dumped for a younger, more awestruck model when the husband gets the degree. The wife did all the work, and someone else gets all the goodies. You might do well to wait, and while doing so, finish your own education. That way you both come to the altar enriched in more ways than one.

Beware if he has recently (in the last seven years) filed for bankruptcy. Sometimes, due to severe medical bills or some other disaster, people have no other remedy. But it is usually a sign of an inability to handle money.

If a person has had bankruptcy in his past and has overcome it by restoring his credit, you are on more secure ground. He has proven his character and integrity by taking care of his poor management or unfortunate circumstances.

Be careful if he will not discuss finances with you. This reluctance may be due to immaturity, or he may be hiding something. Either way, waiting is the sure cure. Give yourself time to see if his reluctance to be forthcoming and honest with you changes. Take a money-management course together.

Learn how to talk about money without arguing. Get some financial counseling together. Insist on full disclosure *before* the wedding. If he asks you to put all your property or monies in his name, or even in a joint account before you are married, be careful. If you have known him only a short while, you cannot know his true ability to handle money. Talk to his family and friends, and observe carefully. How a person handles money is an important signal. Insist on seeing bank statements and tax returns. Be thorough so there will be no surprises.

6. MR. BITTERNESS

This dude may be habitually bitter, or he may just be having a big bitterness attack. He may still be struggling with unresolved anger or grief. He may be depressed. He may be caught in a spiritual battle. Understanding the roots of bitterness and their real nature takes time. Unresolved bitterness and resentment against family, ex-spouses, children, bosses, and so on can be a huge source of conflict in marriage. We tend to project onto our spouse the issues and feelings we have left over from previous relationships. If your beloved is bitter toward his mom, *watch out*. Find a way to postpone plans until these issues are resolved. Do not assume that your love is so special and so powerful that you will effect a healing that has not happened up till now. You may be wonderful, but no one can do that for another person.

7. MR. BRAIN CHEMISTRY

This fellow has recently been diagnosed with clinical depression, anxiety, or another neurobiological disorder, such as manic depression, panic attacks, ADHD attention deficit hyperactive disorder, Tourette's syndrome, obsessive-compulsive disorder, schizophrenia, or alcohol or chemical dependency. This is not to say that people with these problems cannot be great spouses. They can! But if they are *newly* diagnosed, they probably have some adjusting to do emotionally, physically, and behaviorally. They have to put their major energy into learning about and managing their illness. We both have worked with alcoholics for over twenty years, and would suggest five years of solid recovery and character building before marriage is considered.

You will need to come to understand and accept his illness. This process itself takes time. You may find you are up to the challenge of life with someone who has a neurobiological disorder, and you may not. Marriage to anyone takes energy and commitment. We never know if our spouse could come down with cancer or diabetes or multiple sclerosis. All of these illnesses take cooperation from the spouse in managing the daily routine. The same holds true of someone diagnosed with a neurobiological disorder. There are often support groups, websites, and chat rooms for the friends and family of people with these disorders. You will probably want to avail yourself of them.

No matter how much your beloved tries, he still has an illness that at times will be bigger than both of you. You need to know ahead of time exactly what you are getting into. Love does not conquer all. It helps, but it is not enough.

8. MR. "LET'S DO IT NOW!"

This man at first appears refreshingly energetic. You think: *Wow! He is so spontaneous. Not stodgy like my dad!* All that vim and vigor and enthusiasm sweep you off your feet. His motto is "Eat, drink and be merry, for tomorrow we die" or "Do not put off for tomorrow something you can enjoy today." Delayed gratification is not his forte. He does not like waiting in line, waiting for service, or waiting for sex. He is like a perpetual two-year-old who wants his cookie *now!* He always seems to be in a hurry, almost as if he is desperately afraid he is going to miss something.

You find it almost impossible to resist his charm. You are awed by his logic and find it strangely compelling, at least until you get home. He is the kind of guy who wants to go steady or commit to exclusivity on the first date. Some of these men even propose on the first date. Really insecure, they feel that they must rope you in quickly before you get away. So they press for a commitment that you are not ready for, and when you object, either pout and withdraw affection or complain about your not "trusting" them.

If your Mr. Right is pressuring you for a commitment, watch out. He may be Mr. Right at some point, but it sure is not now. Slow down, make him wait. If he does not, I guess Mr. Not Right Now is Mr. Never Will Be, and it is great that you were given the gift of knowing that before you might have married him.

9. MR. DEPENDENCY

This guy is a close cousin to a fellow we wrote a whole chapter on in our book *Avoiding Mr. Wrong*: Mr. Mama's Boy. Mr. Dependency has some of the same characteristics as Mr. Mama's Boy, but is not so bad as to be a Mr. Wrong.

Clues that your man may be Mr. Dependency:

- Your friends ask you why he still lives at his parents' home.

- He treats his mom too well or terribly.

- He needs his mother's affirmation and approval for what he does.

- He does not understand why you are sometimes jealous of his mom.

- He still expects his mom to make his bed, clean up after him, or make his lunch.

- He wants to include Mom in a lot of your social engagements; he worries when she is alone.

- He tends to focus on people-pleasing and not making waves.

- He has problems saying no or asserting himself.

- He may have poor boundaries and worries about abandoning his mom; he may find making independent decisions painful, or go to great lengths to prove he is independent.

- He may struggle with an undercurrent of anger and resentment, especially toward his father.

A man who struggles with dependency may not be a wimp. He may actually seem hypermasculine and rail against any idea that he is dependent. You can see the dependency, though, in his need to control through withdrawal and pouting or raging.

10. MR. "I HAVE A BAD TEMPER"

This man is not a rage-aholic or a wife-beater. He just does not know how to handle his normal anger. He may be oversarcastic, get depressed, stomp around in a snit, or yell and scream. He is not abusive, just loud. He uses more "you" language than "I" language; that is, he is more apt to say, "You make me so mad!" than "I feel furious." He wants to control his anger but has never learned the skills necessary to do so. He realizes he has a problem, and his desire is to fix it. He just does not know how.

This is the type of man who can benefit from some brief counseling and/or an anger management class. He may grow enormously if given time and opportunity. Not everyone had parents who modeled anger in healthy ways. Some people feel very uncomfortable with their anger but have no clue why it is so troublesome.

A man who recognizes his anger issues and is willing to work on them may one day be a Mr. Right, but he is definitely not Mr. Right—right now. He will be well worth the wait, but you must be willing to wait a very long time for him to find peace within himself so he can be at peace with you.

11. MR. "I AM NOT SURE"

This man is potentially a Mr. Right, but not a good bet in the short run. Some women are attracted to men who are tentative or uncertain. Maybe it is because they are too. In any event, if a man is "not sure" about committing to you, he is *not* ready, and you had best *not* wait.

No woman wants a man to be halfhearted in his commitment. If you have to talk him into it, forget it. There are other men out there. And perhaps if he lives without you for a while, he will see he needs and loves you enough to commit after all. Doubts are a good thing: they point out where we still have work to do. When we work them through and face them squarely, and still want to commit, then we are ready.

So do not panic, just move on. If the relationship is right, he will mature and seek you out. If not, you do not want him anyway.

So, what have you learned? We hope that this chapter has helped you understand that waiting is a good thing and that devotion does not mean rushing. Waiting to resolve issues or to let him grow up or get help will only make your relationship stronger. It is just as your teacher used to say: "Stop, look, and listen . . . and you will avoid being hit by the train!"

CHAPTER 10

RIGHT FOR YOU MAY BE WRONG FOR ME

There are probably some people you have met that you just could not like. No matter how much you tried, they always seem to rub you the wrong way. If you're fortunate you have a friend with whom you clicked automatically, and even over the years, after time away from each other, you could pick up where you left off. And then there are those who seemed abrasive at first, but who grew on you. These reactions are a part of everyday life for all of us. Some people we hit it off with right away, others it takes a while for us to warm up to, and some we never do enjoy.

The reason for this phenomenon is what psychologists call "personality." Personality is a fairly fixed way of responding to the world that we develop early in life. Some say personality is set at birth. That is, you are what you are and you cannot change. Others say personality is not innate, but entirely a product of our environment. Still other theorists believe that some traits are genetic, and others are learned.

All of us have seen babies who from the first hour of their birth wiggle and twist and squirm and are active explorers of their environment, while other babies are placid and still, barely moving a muscle except when distressed or hungry. Some babies are loud, some are quiet. Some are contented, "good" babies, and others are colicky and unhappy. Some are eager to be held. Others seem resistant to snuggles and hugs. In the same family we often see both similarities and differences.

Our interests and the ways our minds work are evidences of personality that surface as we mature. Some of us are quick with numbers and facts. Others are verbal and fluent with words. Some of us like things more than people, while others are energized and in need of the stimulation only other humans can give. Hunger for crowds or the avoidance of them, longing for solitude and silence, a restless sense of adventure, or a quiet serenity are all traits of one personality type or another.

Personality is neither right nor wrong. It just is. God has created us in a variety of ways with a wide range of possibilities. We are capable of using our personalities for good or for ill. People do not do what they do just to make each other crazy—they act and react the ways they do because of their personality types. They may make an effort to curb a negative personality trait from love for someone, but it will probably still be there, even if dormant, for life.

As fallible people, our personalities are "bent" toward sin. We find it easier to do the selfish thing than the selfless thing. Everyone has personality, and everyone has a sin nature permeating that personality. Someday, when the world is restored to God's original ideal, we will see personality in full flower without sin's corruption.

We can see personality differences in the Bible. Peter, Jesus' brash disciple, was of the open-mouth-insert-foot type of personality. He was impulsive, talkative, energetic. He tended to act first and think later. He had strong opinions and great enthusiasm. He could be bold and courageous, or even foolhardy. Yet Peter also was vulnerable to what other people thought. He denied knowing Jesus three times rather than be labeled as one of His followers. Peter succumbed to peer pressure and, along with the Jewish Christians, refused to eat with non-Jewish believers—for which he was later rebuked by Paul.

Paul himself was the strong-but-not-silent type of personality. He did not seem to care what anyone else thought of him. He was head-strong like Peter, but less thin-skinned. He could have a serious dis-agreement with someone close to him and press on as if nothing had happened. (Remember the feud he had with Barnabas about John Mark?) Paul was not embarrassed by his physical deformity or "thorn in [his] flesh" (2 Cor. 12:7).

Where Peter was impulsive and spontaneous (like the time he jumped out of the boat and walked on the water when Jesus called to him), Paul was reasoned and rational. He could use his intelligence to humiliate his opponents, or to challenge his comrades. (See the expoits of Paul in the book of Acts.) Not one to be down in the dumps for long, Paul had a resilient personality. He could roll with the punches and go with the flow, as he related in his letter to the Phillipians. He could prosper and party or he could be alone in a cell. Peter and Paul: two different men; two different personalities.

What about Mary and Martha? The Gospel tells us of these two sis-ters who loved Jesus. They lived in Bethany with their brother Lazarus, and often Jesus came to rest in their home. One day, when He was there with the disciples, Mary sat down at His feet, listening to every word. Martha was scurrying about in the kitchen and finally became so annoyed with Mary for not helping that she complained to Jesus Himself! Jesus told her that she was too busy with many things and that Mary had taken the better part. Those of us who are "doer" personali-ties tend to identify with Martha: "What a lazy sister Mary is, leaving Martha to do all the work while she scandalously sits there at Jesus' feet, with all the men in the room! Why, she has no sense of decency, doesn't even care what's proper for a woman!" Those of us who are more con-templative and less task oriented admire Mary. We say: "Oh, how brave she is, to go against the norms of her day, and sit there right at Jesus' feet! Why, she had her priorities in the right place. Food and drink be hanged. That was the time to be with Him. She is such a role model."

Personality can be seen as a curse or a blessing; a gift or a burden. We can accept ourselves and others and live a more harmonious life, or we can rail, complain, and criticize everyone who is not like us. It is our choice how we respond to personalities: ours and others'.

PERSONALITY AND DATING

What influence does personality have in picking one's future mate? Are some personalities dangerous together? We wonder if opposites really do attract, and if they do, if that is a good thing Why are people attracted to various personality types? Why can some people pick a loser the minute he walks in the door, while others are able to steer clear?

Let's look at some basic types of personalities and how they are similar to each other and different as well. We've used data from *The Myers-Briggs Personality Inventory*[1] to assist us in developing these descriptions of personality types. To make the types easier to remem-ber, we have named them according to the insect they most match.

THE BUTTERFLY
About 28 percent of the population are Butterflies. The theme for this personality is freedom. Butterflies are present oriented. From their point of view, life is short and to be enjoyed. Money should be used freely, and variety is the spice of life. Butterfly types are sensitive to color, smell, sounds, and texture. They would be more interested in candles and incense than poetry. Symbolic stimuli leave them cold.

Butterflies experience life as it happens. They seem to flit from thing to thing or person to person—whatever attracts them. Not apt to have long, drawn-out courting rituals, Butterflies are more into the whirlwind romance. This fits with their high need for freedom. Butterflies are generous, easygoing, and relaxed. Clutter and disorganization are acceptable, though they like to be in charge of the clutter.

In the Butterflies' way of thinking, joy is the reason for living. They have a high need for flexibility and hate being told what to do. They are not hung up with the rules or the "right" way to do something. They are more interested in the process of how things are accomplished than the end result. "Did you have fun?" is a more important question than "Did you catch any fish?"

Skilled at handling challenges and crises, Butterflies are not good maintainers of the routine. They want spontaneity and flexibility. At times they can be unpredictable and get irritated if they are not the ones bringing about a change.

Butterflies are good troubleshooters and can often see ahead to what problems lie down the road. They can move others to action and get their cooperation. They do need helpers, though, to remind them of appointments, schedules, deadlines, paperwork, and issues that need closure. Few Butterflies go to college and even fewer go to graduate school, not for a lack of intelligence but because they do not conform well to school's demands for order and delayed gratification.

Often artistic or musical, Butterflies also enjoy sports and competition. They are always attuned to whether something is fair and equal. They do not like coaches and teachers telling them what to do. They love activities that involve direct participation. Butterflies make good artisans, artists, promoters, entertainers, and crisis managers. They may have a gift with machinery, tools, and sensory materials, especially when used in the creation of something. They may also have a great memory for exact facts, details, and information. They can absorb, remember, and successfully use any number of bits of information that others would overlook.

Usually patient and open-minded, Butterflies are unlikely to be prejudiced. They don't get overcritical of themselves or others. Hence they are good at easing tense situations and facing crises. Their love of a good time, if balanced with sufficient realism and the ability to finish projects, can make them productive, creative, and successful people. But if they do not develop a sense of purpose for their lives and live only for the moment, they will become lazy, unproductive, unstable, and shiftless.

As mates Butterflies are unlikely to break up their unions if they have developed their ability to focus. Their sense of realism gives them a certainty that the grass is not really greener elsewhere and that one choice would most likely be just as satisfying as another. Sexually, they like variety. They are not likely to seek sexual experience with different people; they just want their spouses to be interested and able to provide some variety within the relationship.

THE ANT

About 38 percent of the population are Ants, that is, people whose joy in life is to be useful. These people exist to be productive. They are industrious, stable, loyal, servant-hearted, and patient; thorough, orderly, and good at following through on their commitments. They love tradition, rites, rituals, ceremonies, rules, and regulations. Social responsibility and group loyalty are important to Ants. They enjoy doing the right thing. They like discharging their responsibilities. Frugal and hardworking, they must be able to pay for what they get. They hang out with others who work hard and compliment only people who work hard the way they do. *Work* is the all-important word in their vocabulary.

Outcome is much more important than process to Ants. Thus the question "Did you catch any fish?" is more important to them than "Did you have fun?" They believe that everyone can produce, and indeed ought to do so. They may seem harsh and unsympathetic because they are so focused on being productive. Ants love smoothly run organizations and families. They hate chaos and have a low tolerance for change. Structure, order, and closure are high on their priority list.

In relationships, they can be possessive. With zeal Ants guard their homes, cars, families, jobs, and spouses. Caring for the mate and family is of high priority, and Ants are more apt than other types to be obsessed with making sure family members know the "right way" to do things. Usually the "right way" happens to be the way Ants learned from their parents.

Careful with money, Ants are well prepared for emergencies and provide a stable, secure kind of family life. Their jobs (being productive and doing their duty, remember) are the center of their lives. Family members can be confused by their Jekyll-Hyde tendency, however, in that they can be bitingly sarcastic one moment, and sweet and kind the next.

Ants love to be on time, hate delays, and tend to want others to "get to the point." Since they hate to wait, they may make decisions too quickly just to get them over with. Efficiency is important to Ants, as are structure and planning. They make good administrators, trustees, salespeople, and conservationists. Able to follow instructions and work with the team, Ants are valuable in any organizations in which they chose to be members. Ants are what some call "Rock of Gibraltar people." They are the ones who keep the world going by being steady, reliable, and always on duty.

Ants see sex as a means of release, reproduction, relaxation, and comfort. Often loyal to a fault, Ants are unlikely ever to commit adultery.

THE BUMBLEBEE

About 18 percent of the population are Bumblebees. The word that describes the soul of the Bumblebee is *competence*. Bumblebees are the insects, you remember, who fly, though it is aerodynamically impossible for them to do so! Bumblebees want to have power, mastery, competence over things, but not over people.

Bumblebees love it when you listen to them expound on their well-thought-out ideas. In order to feel good (competent), Bumblebees must always be thinking, designing, figuring things out. They are the visionaries who like models, prototypes, principles, and new ways of doing or conceiving of things. Bumblebees are intolerant of details, however. They hate crises, messes, and foul-ups. Redundancy is odious to Bumblebees. They will find a new way home just for the fun of it. They refuse to believe that anyone (including themselves) should ever make the same mistake more than once.

Bumblebees leave routine plans, details, steps to accomplish, or instructions on how to do something for the Ants to work on. Bumblebees are always inventing, conceptualizing, thinking. They have extremely high expectations of themselves and tend to project these onto others. They give an explanation one time and expect everyone to understand it immediately. If they are forced to restate the obvious, they feel embarrassed because they think others will think they are naive or insulting. For example, a father Bumblebee would never tell a child Bumblebee how to wash the car—he would just tell him to go do it. Father Bee assumes he will hurt the child's feelings if he explains each step.

Bumblebees are possibility thinkers: everything can be changed and maybe should be. They are the ones who see problems and say, "Let's fix them." They may not be aware of the complexity of the task or the details necessary to complete it. They just see what needs to be done. They are able to see the big picture and how things fit together.

Bumblebees are good decision makers and love a challenge. They need to be continually inspired with a goal or a project greater than themselves in order to stay motivated. They see problems as just new opportunities. Traditions and rules exist in order to be changed, from the Bumblebees' viewpoint. They can get impatient if things move too slowly or get too boring. They are able to listen well and follow other people's trains of thought.

Bumblebees are committed to the idea that relationships are important. But they are not natural affirmers. They think that to compliment someone on ordinary, everyday things is to state the obvious. If they said "I love you" when they proposed, once was enough! After that, they believe, their love should be obvious. Bumblebees tend to operate on a highly intellectual plane and may come across as cold and unfeeling. They may appear to be oblivious to their spouses' or children's concerns because of this trait. They have a tendency to hide their feelings behind an imperturbable demeanor. Bumblebees have strong emotions, but they have a hard time expressing them. Personal affirmation from others embarrasses them.

Bumblebees are bored by small talk. They love to talk about ideas, especially new ones, but may put others off by becoming too technical, too terse, or too complex in too short a time.

Financially, Bumblebees are not interested in acquiring great wealth. If it happens, fine, but ideas and principles are more important. They are intrigued by the idea of wealth once in a while but seldom have the patience to achieve it.

Sexually, Bumblebees can be experts in the information/technology aspect of the sexual relationship. Again, learning things is paramount. If Mr. Bee decides it is important to become competent sexually, Mrs. Bee is apt to be quite fulfilled! Bumblebees consider romantic relationships with much thought. They regard promiscuity with disdain, and once they make a commitment, Bumblebees are not the type to move on to another hive, even if their marital relationship is not perfect.

THE PRAYING MANTIS

Fairly unusual, the praying mantis is an insect that gets its name from the fact that it appears to be praying when it clasps its "hands." It is an odd-looking and uncommon creature. Praying Mantis personality types represent only about 12 percent of the population

Mantises are the contemplative ones. Thinking, feeling, intuiting, and self-reflection are all part of the Praying Mantis's personality. They are always pursuing understanding and self-actualization. They are eager to become better, wiser, smarter, more understanding, anything to be all they can be. Personal identity is important to them. They thrive on recognition but dislike competing with others. Praying Mantises prefer to cooperate.

Like the insect, Praying Mantis personality types stand out in a crowd. They are catalysts: they are able to bring out the best in others and motivate people to action. Natural leaders, they get involved with people's lives and growth. They look for the best in others and try to affirm it. Verbally fluent, Praying Mantises are also good listeners who give lots of feedback to others.

They like working through other people in a democratic fashion. Mantises can be persuasive but do not like authoritarian situations. Well able to understand the social climate, they are good at lifting others up and helping them succeed. Praying Mantis types can handle public relations easily and are effective spokespeople.

Although contemplative, intuitive, and thoughtful, Praying Mantises can also be very energetic for periods of time, then full of quiet reflection after.

Generally positive, Praying Mantises keeps their troubles to themselves. They are charming, warm, and supportive in their relationships. They freely express themselves and their feelings. Of all the personality types, Praying Mantises are the most affectionate, loving, dedicated, and sensitive. They are capable of great empathy and may at times let their compassion get the best of them. Praying Mantises are prone to burnout, therefore, because it is hard for them to say no to someone else's needs. Loving harmony and hating conflict, Mantises can go too far to keep the peace. They may be apt to shove things under the rug and just think about them rather than take needed action. They are sensitive to trauma and take conflict very personally.

Praying Mantis types function best when they have a cause greater then themselves. They can be creative, artistic, process oriented. Often they make good writers, journalists, teachers, counselors, pastors, and missionaries.

In the marital relationship Mantises are the experts at being romantic. Romeo and Juliet were Praying Mantises. No other type is as skilled at the romantic, symbolic aspect of sexuality and intimacy. Highly emotional, they are affectionate and tender in their relations with spouse and children. And when fully committed to you, they can be a wonderful and faithful marriage partner.

WHO GOES WITH WHOM?

So, should Bumblebees marry Praying Mantises? Do Ants ever go for Butterflies? If so, is that a good thing? What attracts one person to another, anyway? Are differences helpful because they balance out a couple, or are they the source of most conflicts? Why do some people find they cannot live with each other, yet they cannot live without each other?

While some of the whys and wherefores of attraction between the sexes remain a mystery, there do seem to be some commonalties. Most of us are attracted to others who possess something that we think we do not possess. We have a natural yearning for balance, for symmetry, for equality. If we are thinkers, we intuitively feel drawn to someone who is more emotional, more feeling oriented. If we are shy and introverted (that is, we are more apt to be drained by people than energized by them), we find ourselves attracted to someone who is more extroverted. If we are structured and like schedules, plans, and routine, we may find a spontaneous, playful, flexible person refreshing. If we are slow, ambling, laid-back, and easygoing, we may feel challenged and invigorated by someone who is organized and efficient. If we are daydreamers and love focusing on the possible, the odd, the futuristic, we may need someone who is realistic, practical, objective. So, are we saying that all we need to do to find the best spouse is to track down our opposite? No, it is not that simple. Unfortunately, what initially we find so refreshing and attractive after a while becomes the very thing about the person that irritates us the most. If we do not develop some of that "opposite" quality within ourselves as we mature, and we continue to ask our spouse to carry that quality for us, we are headed for conflict.

In the beginning, the one to whom we are attracted feels complimented and affirmed that we enjoy his personality so much. He likes being Anthony to our Cleopatra, but after time goes on, he becomes weary of carrying our burden for us. What once was appealing soon becomes distasteful.

For example, at first, Susie, more Butterfly than anything else, was flattered that Brad, a combination of Ant and Bumblebee, wanted to make the decisions in their relationship. An adult child of an alcoholic, she had become used to making decisions early in life. A single mom now, she was sick of being responsible for everything and everybody. She longed for someone else to take over once in a while and leave her out of the loop. So it never bothered her that Brad made all the plans, set all the agendas, laid out all the goals for their relationship. Susie was relieved not to have to think about it. It was a pleasure not to have to be the strong one all the time.

Yet as her relationship with Brad progressed, Susie found herself more and more uncomfortable. At first she could not put her finger on what bothered her. Finding herself more irritable and short-tempered with Brad, Susie began to examine the relationship more closely. She realized how what she had found so freeing when they first went out, now seemed stifling. She began to resent what she now saw as his bossy behavior. When he would not even listen to what she wanted to do one evening, Susie blew up. Brad was confused and hurt. He was acting only as he had always acted with her, and now she was angry. He could not figure it out.

Nancy's feelings about her husband, Ralph, went through a metamorphosis as well, but it took much longer than in Susie's case. When they dated and were first married, Nancy thought Ralph's free spirit was invigorating. She reveled in his spontaneity, which was so different from her stodgy Midwestern family. Mountain climbing, skydiving, surfing— all activities she never would have tried on her own—were a breath of fresh air. Nancy and her husband danced, traveled, laughed, and explored the exotic, the weird, the unconventional.

Then, after five years of marriage, Nancy became pregnant. She had a difficult pregnancy and could not understand why Ralph was so reluctant to stop hiking, skiing, climbing, and boating just to be with her. She figured that once the baby came he would settle down and see how important it was to be at home with her and the child. How wrong she was! Ralph wanted Nancy to pack herself, the baby, their tent, and go to the Grand Tetons when the child was only two months old. When she refused to go, he went by himself. He began to do more and more alone, spending money just as extravagantly as he did when they were child-less, even though Nancy was no longer working outside the home.

Nancy began to regard his free spirit as irresponsible and started to complain about it to him. Naturally, conflict ensued. Ralph accused her of being just like her parents: "a stay-at-home party pooper." She accused him of not wanting to "grow up"—and so it went.

You can see in these examples, and perhaps in your own experience, the way attraction of opposites can wear thin after a while. Fortunately, if a couple comes to understand their differences as gifts and not curses, a more contented rhythm can develop. For example, Nancy learned to accept that the man *she chose* was a free spirit, and that all the nagging and cajoling in the world were not going to change him. For his part Ralph began to understand that since *he chose* a woman who enjoyed the outdoors, but also took mothering very seriously and was not apt to run out the door at a moment's notice, he would have to temper his spontaneity somewhat in order to be in a harmonious relationship. Each one had to be willing to give and to bend. They both had to accept rather than try to change each other. This approach is often key in developing a relationship that works as opposed to one that disintegrates.

WHEN YOU ARE TOO ALIKE

Some personality types are like oil and water. They just do not mix well. Some are like a match with gasoline. Some seem to go together like a hand and glove. Obviously (or at least you would think it was obvious), having more things in common than not gives a couple a better basis for a successful relationship. But being too much alike can pose its own set of dilemmas for a couple heading toward matrimony. What if both of you are airheads when it comes to money? Or both of you are equally hardheaded? What if both are passive and quiet? Too much of any one quality can capsize a relationship as well.

Being too alike can offer some interesting challenges. For example, Mary and Ted were both quiet, introverted individuals. Ted was a librarian at the university, and Mary was a music teacher in a small, private school. Both of them came from strict religious homes where the father was the dominant figure. Sensitive and tenderhearted, both of them hated conflict of any sort. They rarely argued and never raised their voices. They abhorred violence and could hardly bring themselves to ask for correct change at the grocery store. Both felt somewhat alienated from their stern parents and were determined to be more warm and accepting with their children.

When little Tad came along, he was soon the center of their world. Reluctant to follow in their parents' paths, Ted and Mary decided to be what some would call "hands-off parents." They rarely rebuked little Tad and never spanked him. Time-outs were unheard of in their home as they let the child do pretty much whatever he wanted to do. When friends commented on Tad's uncontrolled behaviors, Mary and Ted defensively stated that they did not want to "squelch his spirit." In private moments they often shrugged their shoulders when he acted out, saying they did not want to fight with him.

In this case both parents were passive, timid people who hated conflict. They were ill equipped (and misinformed) about how to be "good" parents. Eager not to repeat the harshness of their own upbringing, they went to the other extreme and created an equally dysfunctional home.

WHAT DOES THIS MEAN FOR YOU?

When considering personality factors in a relationship, the following guidelines may help you.

1. GET TO KNOW YOURSELF WELL

If you don't know who *you* are, how will you be able to choose someone who is compatible? What matters to you? What values and morals do you hold dear? What are you looking for in life? Where do you want to end up in thirty years? What drives you crazy or makes you furious? What challenges you and gets you motivated? What type of person do you need when you are sick or injured? Are you much of a nurturer yourself, or do you just expect others to give to you? Are you able to sacrifice for others and put their well-being above your own, if necessary? Do you always need to have your way? Are you a neatnik or a slob? Are you compulsive about anything (food, sex, music, religion, shopping)? Do you abhor alcohol, or do you party with the best of them? Are you affectionate and warm, or more cool and standoffish?

Does the idea of sexual intimacy excite you or turn you off? Are you a fearful or timid person, or are you brash and bold? Are you quiet, bashful, and shy, or are you loud, extroverted, and gregarious? Do you have a good sense of humor? What kind of things make you laugh? Can you take a joke, or are you hypersensitive to teasing? Are you noted for your patience or for your irritability?

In short, are you a Butterfly, Ant, Bumblebee, or Praying Mantis? Or are you a combination of these?

Ask your friends and family members how they would answer these questions, and see if your perception of yourself is how you actually come across to others. The more feedback you can get, the better. There are many personality tests and inventories out there, and any competent psychologist can help you find the ones that are right for you. Objective tests are often invaluable in getting to know ourselves. The wonderful thing about knowing yourself and being at peace with yourself is that you can then relate to and even marry one of many other personality types. You are not limited to only the people who make up for your weaknesses and flaws.

2. Broaden Your Experience in Friendships

Befriend as many different people as possible. Try to understand what makes people tick. Compare their outstanding qualities to yours, to those of your parents, your siblings, your other friends. Do not be afraid to get to know someone who is different. Building a friendship (not a romance) is an important way to get to know someone. You will meet many people who will be good friends over the years, but only a few will be people whom you might marry. The better you are at being a great friend, the better your chances of being a great spouse.

Marriage takes compromise and flexibility, both of which you can learn in good friendships with men. Do not assume every relationship has to be romantic or lead to the altar for it to be valuable. One friend of Meg's took a very creative approach after his wife left him. He had not wanted a divorce and took sufficient time to grieve and heal. Then he decided he would date as many different types of women as he could. He realized that he had made a poor choice the first time out. So he spent time with women who had interesting qualities, some of whom were not the physical type he was normally interested in. He dated tall women (he is short), thin women, fat women, short women; women of color, women blond and lily-white; women who were older, younger, more educated, less educated. He worked hard at being a friend and a gentleman, and when he finally found his wife-to-be, he had learned many excellent skills for friendship and marriage.

While even today most women are hesitant to ask out a fellow, at least for the first date the principle remains the same: seek friends and fun and fellowship first. Keeping a relationship low-key and nonromantic gives you a lot of freedom to explore the guy's personality without a lot of pressure.

3. DECIDE WHAT ATTRACTS YOU TO THE OPPOSITE SEX AND WHY

It may help you to ask yourself some of these questions:

- Do you look only for a great body because all you want is a good sexual experience?

- Do you feel attracted only to men with money because you resent the fact that your parents were poor?

- Do you go after only educated men because you do not think you can make it on your own?

- Do you like weak, passive, quiet men because you want to be the dominant one?

- Are you so used to being abused by someone that you overlook abuse or even find verbal or physical abuse a sign of strength?

- Are you so irresponsible that you are looking for someone to fix you or save you or change you?

- What is the payoff for you to be attracted to certain men and not to others?

- Do strong men scare you? Do weak men repulse you?

- Do only gay men seem safe to you?

- Do some men, especially those who are nice to you, bore you to death?

- What was your father like?

- If you did not have a dad, who is your ideal fantasy dad? Do you see any correlation to the type of man to whom you are drawn?

- What did your mom model for you in how to relate to men?

- Did she respect men or find them stupid? Did she degrade them in front of you or build them up as gods?

- Did she imply that you would never make it without a man, or did she push you to stay away from them?

- Did your parents' marriage inspire you to marry well and forever? If not, why?

- What did their examples teach you about yourself as a woman and about the opposite sex?

Often our family background has a profound influence on the type of personality we seek in marriage. So giving this area some deep thought will be productive.

4. Look at Successful Relationships

Seek out the couples who have been married at least twenty years and still enjoy it. Discuss marriage with those you respect for their hard work in their own marriages. Talk with couples who have come to terms with their differences and are now successfully committed and connected to each other. Learn from the masters of marriage and you will save yourself many tears and avail yourself of many wonderful moments.

5. Talk to Women Who Have Blown It

Ask them what they were looking for and what went wrong. Ask them how they would choose differently today. One of the best questions you can ask them is "What misconception did you carry into the relationship?" So often we are operating off of some very dangerous and destructive assumptions that are common to many bad relationships. It could be that she thought she could change him, or that he would change on his own, or that because he was like her dad he had to be right. Find out what it was that might have led to the poor decisions, look for them in your own ways of dealing with men and be sure you make the needed changes before you create a disaster in your own life.

Look at patterns in your family and extended family. What choices have the others in your family made? How did they fare? What factors influenced them positively? Negatively?

6. Ask Yourself What Kind of Man You Want to Parent Your Children

It is important that if you have kids, you realize that they are a huge part of the union of the two of you. There may be some natural unease or discomfort and adjustment, but there has to be some hope that your husband is going to be able to take on the role of Dad by winning their respect and love. If you die, he is their only parent. You have an opportunity to put someone in their lives with character that will build their character. Or you can give them a father figure who will erode whatever good you have instilled within them. Don't be so selfish that you think of yourself and not them. Especially since Mr. Right is someone who will be a great father as well as husband. The two come together in one package.

Ask yourself some tough questions: If something happens to you, what type of parenting would you want your future children to have? What values do you want instilled in your children? Will this man or that man best give you what you are looking for? In twenty-five years, if this guy does not change, will you be proud of him and how he relates to you and the kids? Would you want this man or that man for a dad if you were a kid?

7. Ask for Feedback

Go to those who know you the best. As we have said before, parents, siblings, cousins, teachers, coaches, and coworkers can be rich sources of information. Often they can see what you cannot about yourself and about the persons to whom you tend to be attracted.

Hearing feedback is always a little threatening. We don't like to hear negative things about ourselves. But if these close people cannot be honest with you, who can? You may think that they do not understand you, and maybe they do not totally, but they may have a piece of the puzzle that you need. What can it really hurt, in the long run, to listen to and consider their thoughts seriously? If nothing else, they will feel complimented that you asked.

8. Learn to Accept Differences

Differences are just that: differences, not personal attacks. Most people who do things differently from the way we do are not trying to drive us crazy. The more accepting we can be now in a friendship or dating relationship, the easier it will be to accept differences in the person we choose to marry. Practice really does make *better* (though not perfect). Desensitizing yourself to differences is a great way to grow and become a more interesting, well-rounded person.

Becoming tolerant does not mean you will never mind any difference, but rather that you will be less defensive when you do run into differences in your married life. We may still prefer broccoli to brussels sprouts, but we can at least appreciate that to some people, brussels sprouts are a treat.

Knowing personality types helps us understand ourselves and each other. But the fact is, whatever your personality type, in order to enjoy a happy and healthy relationship, you must be willing to change, adapt, and tolerate within marriage. Make sure your Mr. Right plans to do the same. Every couple will have moments of conflict. With loving, hard work, though, any couple can discover harmony—and joy!—that lasts over the long haul.

PART III

THE
SEARCH

CHAPTER 11

WHERE AND HOW TO LOOK FOR MR. RIGHT

Why is finding Mr. Right so difficult? Where is he hiding, anyway? And why does it seem as if all the good guys rode off into the sunset?

We have many single female friends and acquaintances who are bright and attractive and who ask us to let them know if there are any wonderful, eligible men in the world. Contrary to appearances, they are there. We call them "men in waiting." Some do not even know they are looking for a lifetime companion, but they are. Some do not know what a committed relationship should look like, but they can learn. You really do not have to hang out at the cemetery looking for men who have just buried their wives (although that is actually a better alternative than what some women choose). The situation is not hopeless, and hopefully we will give you some insight into bumping into Mr. Right.

WHAT ABOUT THE WEB?

Whatever the reason, it does seem difficult for women to make a meaningful connection when they are ready to settle down. One place to which many singles are flocking is the Internet. As we mentioned in Chapter 3, millions of people worldwide are connected to the Net. Just a quick perusal of the available websites for singles is overwhelming. Almost everyone has at least thought about using it. And not just twenty-somethings, either—widows, widowers, and divorced women and men of all ages are surfing along with the kids.

Martha, age forty-three, is one of these. She was widowed, had two kids, and was tired of the bar scene. She posted her picture on one of the largest and best organized Web dating sites along with a paragraph or two about herself. Within hours she had ten e-mail messages from men who were interested in making her acquaintance.

More and more people are finding the Internet to be an efficient matchmaker. Match.com, one of the larger sites, has more than 2.5 million subscribers.[1] Blacksingles.com debuted in 1998 and had three thousand check-ins in the first month alone.[2] Some sites are free. Others charge a nominal fee, while a few are quite pricey. For example, It's Just Lunch charges about $1,000 for a carefully screened list of introductions.[3] Other sites will charge you much, much more and deliver nothing, so you have to be cautious if you look to the Web as a source for potential partners.

One of the sites we have examined is Eharmony.com. Clinician and author Neil Clark Warren developed this site. He did not just set up a bulletin board for singles, he created a matching tool that links people who have similar values and things in common. Just taking the site's personality test can add insight into who you are and for whom you are looking.

People can use the Web not just to find dates, but to find companions. They are clear about their intentions ("I just want someone to attend the theater with") and find new friends who enjoy similar interests. But axe murderers like to play tennis too. Some rapists just love the theater. So before you go on-line and invite someone into your life, you need to be sure you have done everything you can to ensure that he is on the level.

The fact is, pornographers and pedophiles use the Net. Did you know that in June 2000 police arrested the first Internet serial killer?[4] U.S. News reports that one organization alone receives 650 on-line stalking complaints every day.[5] Counselors are reporting an epidemic of men and women who suffer from on-line porn addiction. Financial scams, hacking scares, identity theft, and adoption rip-offs have all happened to real people using the Net.

Yet the fascination is there. Millions of singles are seeking partners on-line. Some see Internet dating as a way to build up a level of intimacy with minimal risk. Internet courtship depends a lot on one's verbal fluency and the assumption of honesty. And that is where the rub comes. How can you measure how honest an unseen correspondent is being with you? Since there are no visual clues available, it is easy to minimize the weight one is carrying or exaggerate how much one loves working out. The annoying nasal quality of one's voice, or the lisp with which one speaks, or the other defects, disabilities, or odd characteristics that would strike someone at an actual meeting go unreported.

In one way, this fact is a good thing: it allows people to establish a relationship based on thoughts and feelings, character and personality, rather than on outward physical characteristics. Yet *all* of this still assumes honesty at some level. While a few couples have found wedded bliss via the Internet, not all such encounters have ended happily. The media has widely reported cases of murder, rape, or abuse that flowed from an Internet connection. So we strongly recommend caution: know what you are doing and do not be naive. An Internet relationship cannot provide real intimacy. It is just the beginning, sort of like saying hello. You would never marry someone after just saying hi, so do not assume that a year's worth of Internet e-mail substitutes for reality.

If you want to consider the Internet as a place to legitimately meet someone, you need a place that is safe and provides a solid screening process. Unless you use a service like Eharmony.com, which meticulously screens each applicant, you are taking a chance every time you give out your e-mail address. One woman found that the person she was matched with actually lived in her apartment complex, and when she checked him out with neighbors she found that he had lied about his education, his smoking habits, and his alcohol consumption. This deception is not as rare as you might think. Even naturally honest people are apt to exaggerate their good points and minimize their defects on-screen. Some people have gotten so disillusioned that they have abandoned the Web altogether as a means of finding Mr. or Ms. Right.

Here are some tips for safely surfing the Web in search of Mr. Right.

RESEARCH THE WEBSITE CAREFULLY

Get references from some of the women who have used the site. Any reputable site will have success stories and satisfied customers. Ask your on-line service about any complaints they may have had about a particular site. Notice what type of image a dating site projects and discern whether the type of person *you* want would sign up at such a website.

MAKE SURE YOU REMAIN ANONYMOUS

Most reputable sites do not give out your actual e-mail address to interested parties. You choose a code name and the service forwards any e-mails to you. Be careful not to reveal your phone number or address or other identifying information.

TRUST YOUR GUT

If something feels weird, chances are, it is. If an on-screen relationship seems to be working, talk to the guy on the phone before you meet him. If you get bad vibes on the phone, do not expect your experience to improve in person.

PRESENT YOURSELF HONESTLY

Write your introductory paragraph carefully but completely. Watch your grammar, punctuation, spelling, and language. Sloppiness is a turnoff. Make your profile unique and avoid clichés. Most everyone likes sunsets, walks on the beach, and snuggling, so you need not mention them. Make your profile positive, brief, but honest. You do not need to give the story of your life. Focus on your strengths and be upbeat.

THINK TWICE BEFORE POSTING A RECENT PHOTO

You never know where that photo might appear. Your head shot just might show up on the shoulders of a nude body. It could also be used to identify you by some pervert who is looking for his next victim to stalk. Be sure that the site you use takes all their people through several safety filters before you transfer or post a photo.

ARRANGE MEETINGS WITH CAUTION

If you decide to meet the person you have been corresponding with, be careful. Meet in a public place during the day, and even consider bringing a friend. You can encourage your e-mail friend to bring someone too. Or you may just have your friend hang out in the same restaurant or coffee shop to keep an eye on you in case you need to bail. Do not get in the man's car or go to his apartment or a hotel. Let someone else know exactly when, where, and with whom you are meeting so he or she can make sure you arrive home safely.

If it is clear that your correspondent has deceived you or is just not going to work for you, say so, and quickly. Excuse yourself and *leave*. Do not be afraid to make a scene if something happens that frightens you—better safe than sorry.

Go Slowly!

Even if the first meeting or date goes great, do not leap in with both feet. Use the same common sense you would if you had met the dude at work or at church. Corresponding on the Internet can create a false sense of intimacy. As we have stated, it takes at least three months for a face-to-face crush or infatuation to wear off, and one based on an e-mail association may take as much as a year. Even then, a year's worth of e-mail is no substitute for a good six to nine months of actual conversing in person and spending time together.

OTHER PLACES TO LOOK

Let's say you have tried the Web with no luck, or you just are not ready for a cyber-relationship. What is a decent woman to do when she wants to meet Mr. Right? Once she has worked on herself to become as Ms. Right as she can be, what is the next step?

It may seem trite, but it is true: it is *whom* you know that counts. Most family and friends are still a great source of contacts for the woman looking for Mr. Right. You may find that someone at your office has a cousin or an uncle or a brother who would be worth getting to know. Let your coworkers know you are open to dating. You never know if somebody's stepbrother might be your Mr. Right.

If you meet someone at the office, make sure you know your company's policies about coworkers dating before you give your heart away. It would be tragic to lose your heart *and* your job. Certainly the workplace gives you a good opportunity to see a man in many different situations, under various stresses and pressures. You can probably get a pretty accurate picture of his character by his behaviors and attitudes at work.

If you do date someone from the office, do so discreetly. Do not flaunt the relationship in front of other coworkers, and maintain your professionalism at all times. Your personal life should remain separate from your work life. Married couples can and often do work together, but they are savvy and wary of boundary violations that can wreak havoc on a work environment.

Where the boys are is not always obvious. Place yourself in a spot where there are lots of men. While college campuses are more female dominated these days, they are still one of the best places to meet men. Whether as a full-time student or as a sixty-five-year-old woman taking a gymnastics class in the evening, if you have a college nearby, it can be a great source of interesting and interested people. Check out activities that attract men. If you are an artsy type, go for the artistic endeavors: painting, acting, writing, woodcrafts, architecture, or sculpting. If you are a technocrat, look into endeavors such as web page planning, attending classes on the latest computer technologies, teaching computer classes at the local university night school or the YMCA. If you are an athlete take up a new sport: sailing, tennis, bowling, bocce ball, car racing, golf, or swimming on a local adult swim team. Even if you are a non-sports type, you can still learn enough about various sports men enjoy to converse intelligently. (Don't fake interest, but do learn enough to be knowledgable.) All of these activities can lead to new acquaintances and unique ways to spend time with a prospective fellow.

To increase your odds, you might check out the occupations and situations where men predominate. For example, there are still more men than women in the military, seminary, and certain high-tech fields. More men are in the construction, agriculture, and engineering fields. Certain parts of the country are heavily male populated, such as Alaska. As we said above, certain sports seem to attract men: skeet shooting, hunting, target shooting, car racing, horse racing, football, and baseball. Another area you might consider is taking a course in car maintenance. Go hang out where the men are. Even if you are only there to watch and cheer for your home team, you might meet someone on the sidelines of that company softball game. You could always bring the snacks and really make them notice you! Get interested in things that men like. (Remember, do not fake an interest, develop one you already have. See Chapter 3 for ideas.)

Finding Mr. Right may be a challenge, but it is one for which you can gear up. You are worthy of finding Mr. Right. You do not have to settle for anyone who comes along. You can optimize your chances of finding the spouse you need. Looking around is just the beginning.

For every setting we mentioned, there are at least twenty more that you could list that are in your community. So we invite you to do just that. Stop and list the things you could do, the places you could go, the classes you could take, the hobby you could start, the groups you could join. You *could* do a lot of things, but *will* you? Something inside of you must click and help you see that it is your job to make the contact, not God's or your sister's or anyone else's. If it is time to get down to the business of relationships, make the list and then experiment with the places and activities you have identified. He could be out there signing up for that gymnastics class right now.

CHAPTER 12

IS IT OKAY TO FLIRT?

Perhaps the very question of whether or not flirting is acceptable be-havior offends you. "I don't flirt," you say. "Flirting is manipulative, insincere, old-fashioned, and deceitful. I would never do it. Men think women who flirt are cheap!"

Let's consider an example. One of the best flirts we know is thir-teen months old. She is sassy, exuberant, natural, and gets almost any-thing she wants with her six-tooth grin, her big, blue eyes, and her charming giggle. Babies are the best flirts. They have to be. If they could not flirt, they would never get much attention. You see, flirting is merely nonverbal communication. We all do it. It is just a matter of how well and how consciously. As babies we all did it naturally, but by young adulthood, we have learned to suppress and even be repulsed by it.

Some Christians believe *flirting* is a dirty word. They think that to flirt is to play mind games, to manipulate, and to play the coquette. Is that idea true?

Perhaps a more accurate way of asking if it is okay to flirt would be, "Is it okay to attract a man?" The answer is yes! Flirting is an alternative way of connecting, of socializing effectively, and of sending others a positive message about your availability. It is a way of testing the water to see if the other party is interested in swimming, without getting too wet at first!

Is it deceitful or insincere to admit you are interested in someone? Flirting is only as manipulative as you make it. It can be fun, innocent, amusing, and helpful. The good flirt takes control in a positive way and uses her feminine power without being controlling or dishonest. She treats flirting as what it is: putting her best foot forward and attempting to get a man's attention in as non-threatening a way as possible. It's fun, it's natural, it's easy. And by all means, it is okay!

WHAT KIND OF FLIRT ARE YOU?

Put aside your hesitancy and give the idea a chance. Here are several types of flirts. See if you can spot yourself. First, let's look at the type of flirts no one wants to be. Beware if you see any of your own flirting styles here!

THE RELUCTANT FLIRT

At the coffee hour after church, you spot a drop-dead gorgeous man, and you

- keep your eyes straight ahead and stare intently at the paintings on the wall.

- wish you could think of something to say but just grab your coffee and go sit in the corner.

- maintain your policy of not speaking first to a man. After all, if you said hello, he would think you were being pushy.

- can't decide what to do, so you wait to see if he sits near anyone you know. But you lose your nerve and go sit by yourself.

THE OBNOXIOUS FLIRT
At a friend's Christmas party, you

- rush over to the first man you see and try to pull him under the mistletoe.

- gush compliments to any man who says hello.

- seductively hug every man who walks in, to be sure they all feel welcome.

- stand close to an attractive man in line for the food, and follow him to a table whether he invites you to do so or not.

- pretend you know nothing about whatever he is talking about so as to boost his ego.

THE ME, MYSELF, AND ME FLIRT
At a church dinner, you meet a man who seems interested. You

- talk nonstop about your childhood and your family, where you went to school, your job, and all of your hobbies.

- talk about your theological view of the pastor's sermon.

- wow him with your astute knowledge of the Bible and your deep spiritual insights.

- offer advice on how he can get the coffee stain out of his tie, being sure to highlight all your homemaking skills and your love of cooking.

THE COME-ON-STRONG FLIRT

Anytime you spot a delicious-looking man, you

- make sure to lick your lips, stare right at him, and smile seductively. Imagine what it would be like to dance with *him*.

- go right over and put your arm in his and say: "Hi, Gorgeous! What are you doing here?"

- yank on your blouse so your cleavage shows, saunter slowly in his direction, and accidently bump into him.

- make sure you walk by where he is seated on your way to and from the ladies' room, swinging your hips. Turn around and give him a wicked little wink.

THE OBLIVIOUS FLIRT

You are standing at the book table at a large singles convention with a girlfriend, looking at the books. A tall, nice-looking man comes up and asks if you know of a good place to eat lunch. You

- hand him a map of local restaurants.

- start talking to the clerk about a book on the table, completely ignoring him.

- tell him you are from out of town and haven't got a clue.

- point to the information booth and suggest he ask someone there.

THE THINK-IT-TO-DEATH FLIRT

You are at a pool party at your apartment complex. You see that guy who lives down the hall sitting all by himself. You

- wonder why no one is talking to him. He is so cute.

- remember all those great opening lines you read in *Cosmopolitan* and try to imagine how he would answer each one.

- wander around the pool area, pondering what to say. By the time you decide on something, he is already in the pool with two other women.

- stare longingly in his direction and wonder what he could possibly be thinking about. If only you were good at mind reading!

Now that you've seen the big no-no's in flirting, what *should* you be aiming for as your own personal style?

THE MILLENNIUM FLIRT

You are paired up to teach Sunday school with the new guy from Colorado. You

- make sure you position yourself where you can catch his eye naturally and easily. You don't stare but catch his gaze, and look away with a smile.

- focus on him when he is talking. You act interested, not fawning. You are sure to look him straight in the eye when he says something especially important or interesting.

- smile appropriately and maintain an upbeat outlook as you work together. You make sure to have a twinkle in your eye and a laugh ready at all times.

- keep your body posture open and relaxed, leaning toward him as he speaks, and leaning slightly back as you speak. You tilt your head naturally to the side as you listen, and speak clearly when you talk.

So, what type of flirt are you?

FLIRTING IS FUN!

Even if you feel clueless about flirting, you can learn to enjoy it. Flirting is the conversation starter of the new millennium. Successful flirts have learned to put others at ease with a smile and a sincere interest in the other person. You do not have to be a "sexy babe" to be a good flirt. In fact, many beautiful women are failures at flirting because they are too aloof, too stuck on themselves, or too plastic in their appearance. Flirting is a skill that we all had as babies. It can come naturally again, if we are open to accepting ourselves and enhancing our understanding of what other people are looking for and what makes them feel comfortable. All we need is to learn a few simple concepts to keep rejection at a minimum and friendliness on the increase.

Here are some cut-and-dried principles that are much more practical than theoretical. Check them out.

FLIRTING HELPS YOU GET NOTICED

One of the main reasons animals and humans flirt is to be noticed. Male birds, especially peacocks, love to preen and prance, showing off their finery, hoping to attract the best female in the group. They want the female to notice them, not to be scared of them. They want to attract the female, bring her closer, make her interested.

Humans do it too! And not just males. When a woman makes slow, rhythmic movements with her hands—twisting a necklace, stroking her hair, or smoothing a skirt, for example—men read that as a romantic gesture. Just as animals have certain nonverbal signals that are translated as "I'm interested" by the opposite sex, so we humans give signals too. Another example: When a woman rubs her thigh or her knee while sitting, or rubs her neck or collarbone while standing, she is giving off a clear signal that she is interested in the man she is with.

SMILING IS FLIRTING

Smiling is contagious! If I smile at you, you are much more apt to smile at me! No one is attracted to a glum-faced individual. People who smile more are perceived as happier, nicer, friendlier. Are you a ready smiler? Do you have a scowl or a slight smile on your face most of the time? Even a beautiful woman who frowns or is sour looking is less attractive than a plain Jane who smiles warmly and sincerely.

Everyone warms up to a person who smiles at him. The fact is, when we smile, we feel happier! How you smile is important. Take a good look in the mirror: try on your normal smile. Are you tight-lipped or showing a lot of gum? Are your teeth clean? Do you look attractive, or like the Cheshire cat? (Most people tend to keep their lips too tightly closed. Opening your mouth, even if you wear braces, is always the best approach. It does not mean you will automatically insert both feet!)

Does your smile seem sincere? Does your mouth turn up easily at the corners or does it resemble more of a ghostly grimace? Smiling is an art, and it takes more than saying "cheese" to get it right. Practice in front of a mirror. Ask your friends for feedback. Look at old photos. Notice people you are attracted to: what kind of smiles do they wear?

Your eyes are an important part of your smile. Did you know that? We all know what it's like to meet someone who has a sparkle in his eye. We say of someone jovial that "his eyes twinkle." When someone is attracted, we often say, "He only has eyes for her." When someone is in love, we say, "She has stars in her eyes." Let your eyes shine. Eat well, drink lots of water, and if you drink alcohol at all, don't drink much. Get lots of sleep. No one is more unattractive than someone trying to turn a yawn into a smile!

Your goal in smiling sincerely is to pass on a sense of happiness, well-being, and safety to others. It is a very simple and natural way to flirt.

COLORS HELP YOU FLIRT

In the animal kingdom, it is the males who flash the colors. Fortunately, women get the advantage in the human arena. What do colors say about you? What colors are attractive? What colors are clues to a man that you are available and interested?

Remember that the purpose of makeup is to enhance your good features and draw the focus away from your less-attractive ones. In our day and age, red is an exciting sexual color, especially to men. It is the color of attention: stop signs, fire trucks, traffic lights that mean *stop*, and fire are red. We use blush to redden the face, to look healthy and vigorous. When we are sexually aroused, our fingernails and face redden due to increased blood pressure. Perhaps that is why a woman intensifies the attraction with red makeup! While our focus always needs to be on the inside, we should not shy away from doing the best we can with what we have in making ourselves look more attractive.

FLIRTING SAYS, "WELCOME!"

To flirt is to put out the welcome mat to a man. It is one thing to get someone's attention. It is quite another to make him feel comfortable and welcome. Men are very sensitive to the clues women give out about whether or not they are approachable. We can laugh all we want to about the "gal with the 'come hither' glance," but she is the one who has the dates. In the beginning stages of flirting with a man, the goal is to make him feel welcome, not threatened. Men, whether they admit it or not, are very soft in the ego department. They do not like to be rejected. So they need very clear signals that it is okay to approach a woman. (See Chapter 2 under the subhead "She Is Approachable" for ideas.)

TWELVE FORMS OF FEMININE FLIRTING

This may seem obvious, but there is a right way and a wrong way to flirt. Flirtation is very different from sleaziness. Flirtation is the art of making yourself an attractive, friendly woman without saying a word. Later stages of flirting can involve words, but the first steps are nonverbal. What do we mean? Remember what your mom always said about first impressions? All of us size up others in a split second based on appearances. Fair or not, how we appear often sends unintended messages. For example, if you walk, talk, and behave like "one of the guys," don't be surprised if they don't see you as a woman. Guys may not be good at nonverbal communication, but they are attracted to a woman who acts female! Women can be strong *and* feminine.

What are the signals that are culturally feminine? Here are some:[1]

1. LEAN BACK

You may find that you do this naturally when you are around a man in whom you are interested. Shifting your hips forward and leaning slightly back when sitting, standing, or walking projects femininity. Be careful not to slouch. People who stand up straight exude confidence, which is more attractive to both sexes. (How attracted are you to a guy who is slouched down in a chair, with his arms hanging limp at his sides?)

2. Touch Your Face, Neck, or Leg with a Flexible Wrist

Men tend to move their hands in a stiff, full-palmed manner. Women tend to be more limp-handed. You may never have noticed this fact, but it is amazing how common it is.

3. Gesture with Your Palms Up

Have you ever noticed how cats and dogs will turn over on their backs and toss their feet in the air as a sign of submission? They are communicating friendliness, that they are not a threat to you. In the same way, when women gesture with their palms up, it is a nonverbal cue that they are safe, non-threatening, or open to assistance. Recent research has shown that the majority of women and men like the idea of a man being a woman's protector, despite the recent suggestions to the contrary![2] So communication of openness to assistance or vulnerability is a very attractive quality in the dating arena.

4. Keep Your Legs Closed

What your mom told you was right: it is more ladylike to keep your legs together—and it's sexier too. Young girls often misunderstand about this. They need to know that if a guy is looking for a cheap thrill, he will be attracted by seeing skin. If a guy is looking for a relationship, he will want to see character. No real man wants his woman to appear easy. Fashion models often exaggerate the legs-together walk by putting one foot directly in front of the other, while leaning back slightly. This style of walking also creates a slight sway of the hips, which men find alluring.

5. Take Small Steps

Large steps appear more masculine and are better used when walking *away* from an encounter, while small, more diminutive steps are considered more feminine by both women and men. Larger steps show strength but smaller steps say, "Hey, look at me, I am like fine, delicate china!" If you want to appear feminine, take smaller steps as you approach your intended, and larger as you walk away (showing you can get along without him). If you don't mind looking like an old terra-cotta pot, come lumbering in any way you please! Just don't be surprised if the guys treat you like one of them rather than like a gal!

6. Keep Arms Close to Your Body, Swing from the Elbow

Some women may find this an awkward switch to make, but it is important since men interpret arms swung from the shoulder as aggressive and masculine. On the sports field, swing from the shoulder all you need to, but if you want to attract men, learn to swing gently from the elbow when off the field.

7. Stand with Elbows Turned in Toward Body, Palms Down

Men are almost physically unable to stand in this manner, so it is considered a very feminine gesture. If you watch a group of men standing around, you will notice that they stand with their elbows thrust outward and palms down. Obviously, you don't have to do this all the time, but it is useful to try when there are men around you want to attract. To grasp the significance, put your hands on your hips with your elbows out to the side. That is a very male position that tends to intimidate. Straighten out your arms, put them to your side with your palms down rather than facing upward. It is a subtle difference but, combined with other slight changes, it does make a difference.

8. Stand with One Hip Higher (But Do Not Put a Hand on It!)

Standing with one hand on the hip, especially with one hip lower than the other, communicates an "attitude" or self-centeredness; but standing with hips at different levels is very appealing to men.

9. TILT YOUR HEAD, EXPOSING YOUR NECK

Did you know that a long, graceful neck is very attractive to men? That is why the tossing-the-hair move is so sexy. Tilting your head to the side with a nice smile is also winsome. Exposing the neck or emphasizing it with appropriate necklaces is another way of signaling nonverbally. Necklaces exaggerate the length of the neck. Remember: less is more. Too much jewelry or too much neckline signals the opposite of what a woman looking for Mr. Right wants to communicate.

10. USE FEMININE HAND GESTURES

Females tend to move their hands differently than males. Men move their hands in a chop-chop, angular manner. Women tend to keep their hands closer to the body, and move them in a circular motion. Circular movements subconsciously remind men of a woman's curvaceousness, whereas angular movement comes off as aggressive.

11. TURNS HANDS AWAY FROM BODY, PALMS DOWN, WHEN CHECKING NAILS

Men, if their mothers taught them to check their nails at all, tend to turn their palms upward and bend the fingers in toward the body. While this is not one of the more important gestures, it is a way men and women nonverbally signal or communicate their gender differences.

12. CHOOSE THE KNEE-OVER-KNEE LEG-CROSS POSITION

Both women and men use the knee-over-knee leg cross, but when a woman does it, it shows off her legs, especially when she puts her hand on the upper knee. Generally, to show femininity, avoid the position where your ankle rests on the thigh of the other leg. This is a more masculine pose, and women should use it only when wearing slacks and wanting to demonstrate strength or power.

There are many other gestures that communicate availability and interest, but these twelve are basics. Again, when in the workplace, school, or athletic field, it is good for women to know how to show strength, intelligence, dominance, and power. In flirting, however, the goal is not to overwhelm a man with aggression, but to attract him with the mystery of femininity.

CHECK YOUR STYLE

Opposite genders attract for a reason. Men don't want a woman who is just like a man. They want a womanly woman. This desire on their part does not mean every woman who wants to be attractive to a man needs to be gorgeous, voluptuous, or even pretty. Attractiveness has to do with the nonverbal cues you give, not the physical beauty you possess.

Your manner of dress is part of this equation. You do not have to wear lacy, fluffy things to appear feminine, but obviously, a pair of clunky hiking boots, baggy jeans, and a loose sweater are not going to reveal much about your femininity. Many styles of clothing allow the feminine to be perceived: classic styles, tailored looks, avant-garde, and sporty clothes can all be very feminine. Your look will depend on your personality, body type, and preferences.

Remember, however, that what is fashionable at any one time may or may not be pleasing or attractive to men. Women tend to dress in style to impress their female friends and forget what men find attractive. Just because a certain color is "in" does not mean it looks good on you, or that guys like it.

Men like simple: they like the hint, the suggestion, the intimation of femininity, not the bawdiness of revealing too much. Only men interested in a cheap thrill want a woman who is an exhibitionist. The shadow of something is always more alluring than the thing itself.

How you dress does communicate who you are, whether you like it or realize it or not. Clothes make the woman, as well as the man. That doesn't mean you have to shop at Saks. Bargain basements and outlets can often be sources of great looks for women who are wise shoppers.

Challenge yourself to look at your style and evaluate your nonverbal communication with men. Ask friends how you come across. Pay attention to your body language. What messages are you transmitting? What do your posture, stance, and walk say about you? What can you improve? What can you learn from others? It is up to you what message you send. It is never too soon or too late to evaluate!

FLIRTING RITUALS

What behaviors help build rapport quickly? Psychologists who study various cultures and groups have noted certain actions that seem to establish relationships well. Here are a few.

MIRRORING

As counselors we see this one all the time in ourselves and our clients. All of a sudden you notice that both of you are sitting with your legs crossed in the same way, with the same degree of lean to the upper body. You both are speaking at the same rate of speed with about the same tone. When we are tuned into someone else intently, we tend to unconsciously mirror his behavior. If he uncrosses his legs, or stretches, or yawns, we do as well. Mirroring communicates two messages: "I like you and am in sync with you" and "I am similar to you. We have something in common." Remember, imitation is the sincerest form of flattery. Mimicking your date's gestures may not seem romantic, but it communicates that you are "with" him, tuned into him, and paying attention, without saying a word.

Here is how it works: Joe and Sue meet while on an outing with a group of their friends. While sitting in a relaxed restaurant atmosphere, Joe is sitting in a chair drawn up with others in a small circle. Instead of standing in front of him or to the side, Sue gets down on his level by taking the seat next to his. He has placed his mobile phone under the chair, so she does the same. Sue turns her body toward Joe and assumes the same general posture he is exhibiting. She tilts her head slightly to the side as she begins to speak, looking him in the eye. Then she notices that he does the same, mirroring her head tilt. She glances his way again, smiling. Joe turns more toward her, mimicking her turning toward him. Now their knees are touching ever so slightly at one side as they converse. Joe leans back a bit, perhaps trying to take in this new closeness. Sue does the same, all the while smiling appropriately. Soon he relaxes and begins to lean in toward her. Sue lowers her voice to a more quiet, private, hushed tone. Without even realizing it Joe lowers his voice to match hers. And one more evening is begun, with most of the communication nonverbal.

Mirroring is meant to be a very subtle behavior, and in fact most of the time we are unaware we are doing it. This means you should not try to imitate your intended's every nuance or gesture.

You certainly do not want to imitate any annoying or negative traits. If your date is chewing his fingernails, you don't need to do the same to show that you are in sync with him! The goal is to reveal subtly that you are interested in him, not to embarrass him by aping his behavior.

Saying Hello

Getting started is probably the most difficult part of flirting. You have twenty things in your head all ready to say, but by the time you work up the courage, the moment has passed. Open your mouth and begin, even if you feel awkward. Everyone feels that way at first. After all, you talk to strangers all the time, you just don't notice it!

You may laugh and say "No way! I am the proverbial clam. I never initiate conversations! I am too shy!" Sorry! You are mistaken. You speak to strangers every day: the grocery clerk, the gas station attendant, the nurse or doctor, the policeman on the corner, the post office clerk, the hairdresser at the new salon, the UPS delivery guy, the waiter at a restaurant. We speak to these unfamiliar folk all the time but usually discount the conversations because we do not plan what we will say. We feel safer in these interactions because we perceive them to be less risky.

So we save our best, most charming selves for that "special person" who never seems to show up, all the time passing up a chance to charm all of the people around us. Yes, it is less risky to talk to someone in whom we have no interest romantically, but we waste wonderful opportunities to practice our relationship skills, have fun, and maybe even find out that we are interested after all.

Most people are just as nervous as you are about speaking first. Honestly! That's why we all get into elevators and stare at the numbers by the door frame, or ride on a bus as if no one else is there at all. Maybe you are afraid to speak up because you think your friendly hello could attract a weirdo or a pathological killer. Remember: effective relating begins somewhere. Finding Mr. Right means you will "kiss a lot of frogs." As long as you go slowly, you will spot the kooks well before they have a chance to hurt you. And being silent keeps you from even beginning the relationship!

Do you realize that men actually hope you will flirt first? Yep, they are afraid, and they desperately want you to give off some sort of signal that you are interested. And even if you are a bit awkward, most people understand the courage it takes to speak up and find the awkwardness charming. Really! It is more real, more honest, and less suspicious than the overly suave, smooth, or calculating approach of the too practiced.

And almost any remark will do! Even if it is a bit silly—as long as it is not rude, sarcastic, or mean-spirited. You would be amazed at the ways people describe their first meeting. Meg's dad met her mom by asking if he could take her picture in her Easter bonnet! He was standing outside the church with his camera, taking pictures of the girls as they came out of church. It worked. They have been married now for more than fifty-three years!

One way to begin to gain the confidence you need is to *begin*. Start today by greeting at least ten people. Your mail carrier, the butcher, the baker, the candlestick maker: people who will recognize you but are not personal friends. Say hello and smile. Make your smile bright, warm, and wide. Let your eyes sparkle and smile too. You may not be on Candid Camera, but someone is surely watching!

SHOWING INTEREST

Once you have his attention and have mumbled hello, what's next? Why, keeping the conversation going, of course. You do that not by talking, but by looking him in the eye and giving him your full attention. Listening is better than good looks and perfume. Men desire (as do women) to be admired, liked, cherished, and loved. They may not show it as emotionally as women do, but they have the same needs. Listening with rapt attention, sincerely, kindly, and without needing to talk him to death is a sign that you are interested. When you show that you passionately want to hear what is on his mind, you affirm his attractiveness and his sense of self-worth.

Men, at least in the first stages of a relationship, tend to want to be front and center. They like their ego to be stroked, and whether this is due to cultural conditioning or genetics, it is a fact of life with the male of the species. When he talks, show genuine interest in what he has to say. After he has had some time to feel you are sincere, he will undoubtedly want to hear what is going on in your head.[3] Then it will be your turn to charm the socks off him.

TEN TIPS FOR FLIRTING

1. **DO IT!**
Get off the couch, get out of the house, and go mingle.

2. **LISTEN TWICE AS MUCH AS YOU TALK**
And don't talk too much about yourself.

3. **SMILE AND SAY HELLO**

4. **NEVER BE RUDE**
Or insulting, sarcastic, or come on too strong. Instead, be kind, affirming, sensitive, and tuned in to him.

5. **LOOK FOR NONVERBAL CUES BEFORE APPROACHING HIM**
Eye contact, smiles, tilting the head slightly, rubbing his arm, or straightening his tie are the cues that say he is open to you.

6. **WATCH YOUR NONVERBALS**
Less touch is better than more in flirting. Don't invade personal space. Let him breathe.

7. **DON'T PANIC**
If he rejects you, don't assume there's something wrong with you. It may just not be a good match. Get up off the floor, and start again with someone new. Finding Mr. Right usually requires a lengthy search!

8. **DON'T OVERLOOK THE FELLOW IN FRONT OF YOU**
He may not be the man of your dreams, but he could be Mr. Right.

9. **ASK AND LISTEN**
Ask open-ended questions, and pay attention to the answers.

10. **BE SINCERE**
Flirting when you are not interested is mean.

Finally, there is one form of flirting that is always a winner. It is becoming the greatest human being you can become, growing in wisdom and confidence as much as possible, and taking care of your mind, body, and spirit. When a man discovers a woman who has invested time and energy in making herself the best she can be, he is naturally attracted to her. Her life is a way of flirting, attracting men, and it works so much better than batting fake eyelashes at every man who walks by!

So flirt, but do so femininely and wisely. It is okay!

CHAPTER 13

TEN MISTAKES
YOU MUST AVOID
(AND WHAT TO DO IF YOU MAKE THEM)

Say you go to the mall and purchase a blouse you think looks great on you. When you get home and try the blouse on again, you discover it is actually not flattering at all. This is frustrating, but your mistake does not shatter the earth or rock your world. We all make mistakes, hundreds of them over a lifetime. And many of them are easily corrected. But there are mistakes that you just do not want to make, ones you cannot simply fix, and one of those is messing with the IRS. Tax cheaters lose their homes, cars, and paychecks, and must account for their wrongdoing. IRS blunders are some of the most painful mistakes a person can make. But guess what? As anguishing as those are, they do not hold a candle to the devastating mistakes you can make when looking for Mr. Right.

If you are dating someone, the following errors are the big ones. They have horrible consequences, yet people continue to make them.

Why? Because they are mistakes of convenience. They are made in a steady boat that someone did not want to rock. And when you make them, they affect you for the rest of your life—they can even ruin it. If you are seriously dating someone and you sense a proposal is coming, slow down, kick off your shoes, and read the following carefully. You do not want to make any of these mistakes.

The problem is, sometimes it is hard to be objective. You might want to enlist a friend to help you figure out if you are moving forward with Mr. Right, or if in reality you are quite mistaken.

TEN DISASTROUS RELATIONSHIP MISTAKES

1. EXPECT THAT YOU CAN MAKE A SILK PURSE OUT OF A SOW'S EAR

You cannot turn Mr. Wrong into Mr. Right, no matter how much you love him. No matter how loving, sweet, sexy, kind, devoted, intelligent, fun, daring, or darling you are, you are not capable of performing a personality switch in someone. If a man is not Mr. Right material, all your love will not change him. It *might* motivate him to change himself, but it will not in itself effect the desired shifts. Do not fall for the idea that your love is so special, so spiritual, so unique, that it will work where no one else's has.

If, when talking of a past relationship, he hands you the line that "she did not understand me," *watch out*. Your integrity is not going to make him honorable if he isn't. Your conscientiousness is not going to make him responsible if he is a bum. Your prayers are not going to make him into a spiritual dynamo if he is spiritually uninterested.

God does answer prayer, but putting yourself in a position that demands God's rescue is unwise. God wants you to grow, mature, and learn to discern rather than plunge ahead and expect all to be fixed by a cosmic Butler who is waiting for you to ring your service bell. We are on dangerous ground if we think God owes us because we prayed, or that we in our finite abilities can pray someone into being something he is not willing to become.

Here is an example: Shawna was a bright, energetic young woman who loved God, her family, and her work. She was a registered nurse and although she worked long hours, she felt a calling to the patients for whom she cared. Shawna had always been the person others went to when they had a problem. She was positive, gentle, and a good listener. Always believing the best about someone, Shawna often found herself cheering for the "underdog." When she met Rudy at work, she immediately felt drawn to him. His quiet, subdued manner seemed to her to mask an underlying pain of some sort.

Rudy was a pulmonary technician at the hospital who worked the same shift that Shawna did. At first Shawna just listened when Rudy stopped by the nurses' station and chatted while he waited on a patient. She learned that his parents were both alcoholics and that he had been responsible for taking care of his younger siblings after his mom died when he was ten years old. He had graduated from high school and worked nights to put himself through his technical training.

After a while, Shawna and Rudy started dating. Most of the time they went dutch, treat since his salary was less than hers and she did not want to put him out. He occasionally borrowed money from her but usually paid it back promptly—at least in the beginning. Shawna ignored the financial end of things because she had so much fun with Rudy whenever they were out together. They would go line dancing, play softball with a coed team from the hospital, or take hikes in the nearby foothills. Rudy loved to eat out, so they frequented many fine restaurants. Sometimes Shawna wondered how he could afford it, but he always acted as if putting his meal on his credit card was no big deal. She paid cash for hers and kept her mouth shut.

One Sunday at Shawna's church, an announcement was made about an upcoming financial seminar for singles. Shawna suggested that Rudy go, and he reluctantly agreed. Shawna was sure that once he had the right information, Rudy would begin to mature in his stewardship of money. He sat through the seminar with her but let her take all the notes, saying he could read hers. Thinking that was logical, Shawna did not pay much attention. She figured he would absorb the most important points by being there.

Three weeks after the seminar, Rudy came to work and told Shawna he had a surprise to show her. Out in the parking lot, he glowingly told her about the "great deal" he had just gotten on this new red Mustang convertible. Shawna was stunned. When she asked how he planned to pay for it, he said he had cashed in his small savings account for the down payment and gotten a loan. Shawna thought she must not have been praying hard enough for Rudy, so she called her prayer hot line at church and put his situation on it (anonymously, of course). She also printed articles on financial responsibility from the Internet and newspapers and left them in his mailbox at work. By this time, Rudy and Shawna had been dating for a year, and she wanted the relationship to move on to the next level. She was worried, though, that she could not depend on him even to pick up the tab when they ate out. It seemed that no matter how much Shawna encouraged or prayed for Rudy, he just did not seem interested in changing his financial habits.

Fortunately for Shawna, she had a close friend who was a counselor at a local mental-health clinic. This friend was able to help Shawna see that she was trying to make Rudy into something he was not about to be. It made Shawna angry, and then sad, that she had wasted a year trying to fix Rudy, but she realized it was better to break off now than marry and be miserable later.

Shawna is the exception to the rule. Her courage was rare and the insights of her friend were lifesavers. If you are walking around with a pig's ear on your arm, follow Shawna's example and realize that it is never, ever going to become a silk purse that will make you proud and happy.

2. Expect to Find Mr. Right in All the Wrong Places

If you are looking for a musician, you are not going to find him unless you go where musicians hang out. If you want a scholar, you had best look in a college or university setting. We have all heard the complaint that "there are not any good men out there," but sometimes the reason you do not find a good man is that you do not look where the good men are. If you want a nondrinker, for example, you probably will not find him at the local pub.

We believe in singles hanging out with singles. But sometimes if you show up at the singles meeting, everyone there is desperate and looking for "the kill." A singles class could be the wrong class. Go where there are singles who are not just meeting to find mates, where the cause is greater than finding another person. When you do that, your chance of finding Mr. Right is greater and you have a lot more fun than you would at the contrived meet-market affair.

3. Expect to "Hook Up" Now and Find Fidelity and Intimacy Later

One of the saddest things we have seen in the last few years is the increase in the numbers of young women who are taking a more casual—even callous—approach to sex. All over the country, young women are throwing out the expectation that sexual intercourse is something to be saved for marriage and deciding it is more important to "have fun" now. Instead of "Eat, drink, and be merry, for tomorrow we die," their mantra seems to be "Eat, drink, and be sexual now, for *later* we marry." Sure, they want to settle down someday. But right now, fun is all that counts. Sex is just an urge, like thirst or hunger, they reason. There is nothing special about it. No one will get hurt, right? Use a condom and all will be fine.

Little do these young women realize that they are setting themselves up for years of loneliness, heartache, and sexual problems. Few
understand that starting to have sexual intercourse at a young age can
be a precursor to cervical cancer, inflammatory pelvic disease, and
infertility, not to mention the fact that they are making themselves vulnerable to various sexually transmitted diseases. Not many realize the
heartache that occurs when they do find Mr. Right and want a pure,
holy, monogamous relationship with him, yet they cannot get the
images out of their heads from past sexual encounters.

Our first sexual encounters are powerfully recorded in our minds.
Bonding certain memories to certain sexual acts and feelings is auto-
matic for the brain. No matter how much you want to get rid of the
memories later, it is not easy to just wipe them away. Ask anyone who
is addicted to pornography or recovering from sexual abuse, and he or
she will tell you how difficult healing memory patterns can be.

Many women say, "Well, if it is good for the gander, it must be
good for the goose." In other words, if men can mess around, why
can't women? This is like saying,"Gee, men die of heart disease more
than women! What can I do to even out the statistics?" There are
some areas in which women need to be courageously different from
men. Just because many men have been blatantly immoral and acted
like animals does not mean that women should lower themselves to
such a standard. The Bible talks about how in the last days, fathers
and husbands and other men will neglect their obligations to home
and family in favor of pleasing themselves (2 Tim. 3:1–9; 4:3–4; Mal.
4:5–6). While this pattern of selfishness has been visible in some men
in all epochs of history, it seems especially obvious nowadays. The
tragedy is that some young women think this behavior is something to
emulate.

If you have a boyfriend, we have a radical idea for you: be sure
that he is a boy who is also your friend. Do not look for random sex-

ual partners; look for a companion for a lifetime. Listen, you will spend the rest of your life with your husband. You will go to bed with him, eat with him, play with him, grieve with him, go on vacation with him, have children with him, go to dinner with him over and over and over again. Get the picture? You are going to experience many things and spend a lot of time together, so we suggest that you commit yourself to someone you enjoy *a lot,* someone to whom you can talk and in whom you can confide. The happiness that results is tremendous.

Sadly, many women marry men with whom they no common interests and no ability to communicate. In fact, the only thing they have in common is that they have had sex together. The resulting emptiness is unbearable. (If this is you, we are begging you to reconsider your future.)

4. Expect Mr. Right to Make up for What Daddy Did Not Give You

Too many young ladies, girls who were neglected by their dads, consciously or unconsciously look for a replacement in the boys they date. They are desperate for male attention because they did not enjoy a warm, loving relationship with their father; either he was not home or he was critical and cold when he was. Brokenhearted that Dad was gone or never cared, these young women confuse sex with intimacy and love. The boy says, "Let's have sex!" They think, *He loves me.*

Nancy is an example. Her dad was a workaholic who also drank too much. Mom was a socialite who dealt with her own pain by staying away from home as much as possible. Nancy was sent to boarding school from the third grade on and so never knew the security of a loving, intact family life. Now in her mid-forties, she is divorced with young children. She struggles with depression, alcoholism, and sexual addiction. Nancy longs for a stable, monogamous relationship, yet every time she meets a decent man she finds a way to sabotage the relationship.

Recently, after a session with her therapist, Nancy realized how much an early decision had scarred her. When she was fourteen, Nancy had started to date a fellow she was crazy about. They had not yet had sex, and then one day her best friend grabbed him right in front of her and started French-kissing him. Nancy stood there, stunned.

She felt hurt, humiliated, and ashamed, but she remembers thinking, *Well, if he does not take a physical relationship more seriously than that, neither will I.* Nancy realizes now that that conclusion, made out of hurt and pain, drastically shaped her future with men and her inability to commit to a permanent marital relationship.

Whether Dad failed to provide money, attention, love, guidance, or some other essential, Mr. Right will not be able to make up for it. While your Mr. Right may be the opposite of Dad, he is not God and he cannot finally replace the father you lacked. As we mentioned earlier, Mr. Right is not going to want to parent his wife—just his children.

Sad to say, the more you expect a man to do what Dad did not, the more you will alienate him. You will repel him. A formula for a sure disaster is to expect an inadequate husband to make up for an inadequate father. Stop and analyze your childhood. If Dad was not there, realize that you may be a sitting duck for a difficult relationship. The least you can do is discuss it with the man you love. You owe it to him. The most you can do, if you suspect a problem, is to seek counseling to help you correct your expectations and heal your past.

5. Get Too Friendly with a Married Man

While this one seems obvious, we still need to affirm it. Today, some women throw themselves at anyone in pants. A wedding ring is no deterrent. Respect for and honor of marriage as an institution has dwindled to being almost nonexistent. Even in these days of feminism and the so-called sisterhood of women, ladies' respecting other ladies by leaving their husbands alone seems old-fashioned or quaint.

Just in case you are not sure, let us list a couple of the disadvantages of having a relationship with a married man. First of all, while gaining a man's attention is flattering at first, a woman finds it difficult not to long for his *undivided* attention. Though there are always exceptions to the rule, by and large, women prefer their man to be exclusively theirs. The idea that he is committed, however insecurely, to his wife and not to you always wears thin. Holidays, birthdays, and special occasions will all take second place to those of his "real" family. Even if you have children by him, the other children will always seem to take precedence. He will constantly check in with them and leave you to go to them. He may spend money on you when he is with you, or even help support your children, but when push comes to shove, you will be on your own.

Second, you never know when he is going to decide that being with you is just "too risky." You may have lots of sex, but real intimacy and commitment are absent. If he cheats on his wife, what makes you think he is faithful to *you*? How many other women have there been over the years when his wife "did not understand him"? Or how many does he have on the string now? If you cannot fully trust him, how can you develop an emotionally intimate bond with him?

Why some women think half a loaf is better than none is beyond us. It certainly is not God's best for men or for families.

Third, and most important, it is wrong. Choose wrong, and you suffer consequences of eternal magnitude.

Finally, only a very sick girl would be attracted to a child-deserting, family-abandoning man. Anyone attracted to a characterless adulterer is in need of a total makeover from the soul outward. Only a foolish woman would ever mistake lust for love.

6. SEDUCE A MAN INTO LEAVING HIS WIFE AND FAMILY

Seducing a man into divorce may make you feel needed, but it is only the beginning of heartache and trouble. Even if he genuinely comes to love you, marries you, and fathers your kids, there will always be the other family to deal with, plus his guilt and shame for leaving them. No one needs more excess baggage. Why ask for it? You may get an ego boost out of believing that you were more attractive to him than she was, but what kind of man lets himself be seduced in the first place? A man of real worth would never succumb to your wiles, no matter how enticing. If he would leave his first love for you when she began to lose her youthful charms, what will keep him faithful to you? Remember, she had the same devotion, expectation, and hopes for fidelity that you do. And look where they got her!

Marilee is a woman who very much regrets a flirtation with a married man. At thirty she was married and had a couple of kids but felt bored and felt unhappy in her ten-year marriage to Jack. When the kids were all in school, Marilee went back to work at a bank and quickly discovered the excitement of flirting with men in the office. In comparison to them, Jack was so ordinary, so stick-in-the-mud; he never told her sexy jokes or made passes at her. He rarely noticed if she got her hair cut or if she found a new outfit that was flattering.

At work, Bob was different. He was suave and good-looking, but that was not what intrigued Marilee. He seemed so sensitive. He noticed her and seemed to appreciate her. He asked how her weekend went and seemed to care what she said. He would wink at her as he walked by her teller station, and appeared to be genuinely interested in her.

Jack was always so pure and wholesome. Bob was much more exciting. He had a sense of humor and was not afraid to be a bit racy in his conversation with Marilee. He, too, was married, but Marilee could tell that he was unhappy. He rarely talked about his family, and after a few weeks she noticed he had stopped wearing his wedding ring. One day, she sensed that he was a little down, so she asked him to lunch. One thing led to another, and before she knew it she had fallen head over heels in love with Bob.

Within a few months, Bob and Marilee were having sex on a regular basis. Soon she began to beg him to leave his wife and marry her. After about nine months, Bob did so. Marilee told Jack that the marriage was over and started divorce proceedings. Jack fought for custody of the children, and because he was a good dad, Marilee let him have it. Besides, she did not want to be tied down with kids in her life with Bob. Once their divorces were final, Bob and Marilee went to Las Vegas and were married in a small, private ceremony.

Everything seemed wonderful at first. Bob was a great lover, and they reveled in their new life. Yet as the months went by and real life came clanging in, Bob and Marilee could not keep the problems of a blended family from impeding their wedded bliss.

His kids did not like her kids, and so they rarely had them over at the same time. Holidays were a nightmare, and Marilee resented the amount of money Bob had to send his ex-wife for alimony and child support. Jack made do without Marilee's financial aid, but she found coping without Jack's support wearing. Suddenly she realized that her new marriage had become as boring and burdensome as her old one was.

One day, over coffee, Marilee confided to her former sister-in-law that she really regretted seducing Bob away from his family and abandoning her own. Bob was not as debonair as he had been during their torrid affair, and he seemed to resent not having time with his children. Marilee's children wanted to have very little to do with her and spent more time with their dad and his new wife. Marilee said sadly, "Well, I thought the grass was greener, but it really turned out to be AstroTurf."

7. Ignore the Fact That Your Background, Beliefs, and Values Are Totally Different

Love is too often blind. Love itself cannot take care of everything. Mad, glorious sex will not make up for differences in religion, ethnic background, culture, language, or spiritual heritage. Counselors universally agree that the more a couple of people have in common with each other, the better their chances for a successful relationship. Life is tough enough even with someone of similar values or background. To add ethnic, cultural, age, religious, educational, or economic differences only complicates an already snarled situation. Not that people are not able to overcome some of these differences. Some can—but even they will tell you it takes lots of work and commitment to do so.

If you are determined to have a relationship with someone who is very different from you, at least do so with your eyes open. Do not pretend that you will not have any problems because your love is so special. Be clear with your boyfriend about your expectations, preferences, and hopes. Hash out your differences before you decide on a commitment, and get lots of feedback from your parents, friends, and a competent counselor. Face facts. "Opposites attract" is a sentimental way of describing a potentially devastating mixture of conflicting personalities.

Be sure you choose a man for who he is, not just to make a political statement. Wrestle with your doubts and fears. Talk openly with each other. Imagine possible scenarios. Spend time exploring the differences. Planning ahead and being prepared for potential clashes wil make them much more manageable when they do happen.

Jackie and Raul are a good example of how *not* to manage this type of relationship. Jackie came from a strict Lutheran background. She had attended private Lutheran schools all through grammar school, high school, and college. A kind, caring person, she wanted to devote her life to teaching.

After college, she moved to Texas. She and Raul met at the Hillsdale School, where they were both teaching. He came from a strong Hispanic family. His grandparents lived in Mexico, but his parents were retired businesspeople in L.A. Staunch Catholics, they were appalled when he mentioned that Jackie was Lutheran, and not only Lutheran, but Swedish-American. His mom had always dreamed of Raul's marrying an Hispanic woman to "preserve the family." She could not imagine a blonde-haired, blue-eyed Anglo as part of their bloodline.

For their part, Jackie's parents were not too thrilled about having a nonwhite person in their family. "What will the children have to face?" her mother asked. Jackie's brother and sister-in-law said they would attend the wedding but would protest her choice by refusing to stand when she walked down the aisle. Her grandmother began to send her inflammatory leaflets about how all Catholics were going to hell and how Lutherans comprised the only true church.

Finally, Raul and Jackie got so frustrated with everyone that they just eloped. They were sure that their love was big enough to carry them through anything. Besides, they reasoned, their families lived far away, and surely they would come around once they had grandchildren. Or so the young couple hoped.

Unfortunately, the marriage has not gone so well for them. Jackie has had little contact with her family since the marriage, and the couple spends most holidays without any extended family. Raul's mom did visit when their son was born and has warmed up considerably. Yet Los Angeles is pretty far from Dallas, and they do not see her much. Raul's dad remains hurt but at least is talking to them again.

Jackie misses the family traditions and Swedish cooking of her childhood. She feels reluctant to bring her traditions into her home now because she does not want to risk the little family connection she and Raul have with his parents.

What about Raul? For him it has been difficult as well. He loves

Jackie, yet misses the warmth of his father's full approval. He is sad when he sees how much Jackie misses her heritage, but feels helpless to do anything about it. He hesitates to bring it up very often so as not to upset Jackie. He tries to be neutral, not emphasizing his cultural heritage too much, but then feels he is betraying himself. Both Jackie and Raul have suffered from bringing two different worlds together.

At times the families' opposition has put a serious strain on Jackie and Raul's marriage, and they wish they had had some premarital counseling to prepare them for coping with it. Though they love each other, neither of them anticipated what a huge difference culture could play in a relationship or how it would cost each of them in the long run.

8. Get Involved with a Man Who Has Already Abandoned a Family

Again, who needs the extra baggage? If a man is so shallow as to have abandoned one or more families before you came along, what makes you think you are so special that he will never leave *you?*

We all want to believe our love is unique, even unparalleled in the universe, but the fact is, if his mother, sisters, and former wives could not make him a responsible person, you are not going to do so either. No matter how wonderful you may be, you cannot make a man more faithful than he has proven to be already. Even if he claims to have "gotten religion" since his last infidelity, has he done anything to make amends to the family he left? Is he any more willing now to put selfishness aside to do the right thing? Or does he think only of himself, his pain, his problems, his needs, and his shame?

Monica met Ralph at church after a Christmas concert. He was all alone and looked sad, and so she walked up and introduced herself. Ralph soaked up her kind attentions like a sponge. He called her the next week, and they ended up going out to the church's New Year's service, then for coffee and cheesecake afterward.

As Monica got to know Ralph, she discovered the sad tale that was Ralph's life. Married at seventeen to a gal he had impregnated on the first date, he got restless and resentful (by his own admission) and left town to join the Navy. As far as the girl was concerned, he may as well have dropped off the face of the earth—he rarely communicated with her once he was in the service. At some point he received divorce papers in the mail. He was not asked for child support, and he did not volunteer any.

Ralph did a tour overseas during Desert Storm, came home, and started dating one of the civilian women at the naval base. Soon they were talking of marriage, and since his stint in the military was almost over, he proposed. Ralph and his second wife were married in a small military wedding officiated by the chaplain at the base. His family could not attend because his dad was ill, so it was a quiet affair with just her family witnessing their vows.

At this point Ralph figured all his problems were solved. He had a promising job prospect when he got out, military benefits would pay for some additional schooling, and his wife continued to work at the base. Everything looked hopeful.

After several years and two kids, Ralph was well established in the plumbing field and making good money. His wife worked part time at the base and tended the children. He played ball with his old Navy pals on Wednesday night and stopped with them at the local pub afterward for a few beers. All seemed smooth.

Ralph's friendship with Wanda, the bartender at the local pub, began innocently enough. At first he would talk about his kids and the wife, but as time went on he found himself confiding more personal frustrations and problems. Work was pretty stressful, now that he had his own business, and he felt unappreciated by his family. Ralph began stopping off at the pub more than just on Wednesday evenings. He just told his wife that he was working late, and she never *seemed* to care if he missed dinner with her and the kids.

Soon the innocent conversations had turned into a full-blown affair, and Ralph decided to jettison the stable life he had had. He sold the business, left his family, divorced, and moved into the apartment above the pub with Wanda and helped run the bar. After a few years, Ralph and Wanda married, but the marriage was a disappointment to him.

He had felt so affirmed by Wanda before they married, and now all she did was nag because he was not working much. Bills began to pile up, and one day Ralph just took off. He moved to Seattle, where he knew no one, and began attending Monica's church. After some months, he was baptized. He seemed to have a change of heart toward his children but still did not want to move back to the East Coast to be near them. Monica was sure that, with her love and understanding, Ralph would mature as a Christian and that their life together would be all she dreamed it could be.

The problem was, of course, it *was* a dream. Even though Ralph's spiritual conversion seemed genuine, little had changed within his heart. He was still the self-centered, small-minded person he had been in high school, just a bit more mellow. His faith helped assuage his guilt on an emotional level, but it did not seem to spur him on to greater responsibility. He continued to drink a bit too much when Monica was not looking and worked only occasionally. Though Monica had over-looked Ralph's previous failings, eventually she could no longer over-look his current irresponsibility. She wanted to marry him, but began to realize that he was not Mr. Right. It was hard for her to accept that her love alone was not enough to change him, but with help from her pastor and others, she was able to break off the relationship. Her love could not save him or their marriage.

9. GET SWEPT OFF YOUR FEET IN A WHIRLWIND ROMANCE

Why does it takes several months to get a driver's license for the first time, and only five minutes to get a marriage license? Some people spend more time researching a new car or a computer than they do the person they end up marrying.

While we probably all know some married folks who wed after knowing each other only a month, and made it work, most people would say not to rush it. Marriage involves the good, the bad, and the ugly experiences and moods and events of life. If we want a successful relationship, we need to know the person we marry in each of those conditions *before* we tie the knot.

Some men are so insecure that they are sure that if they do not pressure you quickly for a commitment, you will never stay long enough to get to know them. Some women are so insecure that they are willing to commit to the first man who shows any serious interest. While whirl-wind romances are fun, exciting, and energizing, they are not based on realistic assessments of the relationship. Not enough time has transpired to test it under fire!

In one of our clinics we dealt with a young woman who was devastated by her choice in marriage. He did not drink, look at porn, or spend all the money they made. On the outside, he was a great guy. But once they were married, which was less than six months after they met, she discovered the fatal flaw of his and their marriage: he kept everything. He was a pack rat. He piled their apartment high with newspapers he would one day read, magazines he would one day look at, and everything else imaginable. At first, she thought it was just an odd quirk that would not get out of hand, but as time went on she realized something was seriously wrong. When she tried to clean up or take the newspapers to the garage or put them in the trash, her husband became furious and even threatened violence. Their romance had been so much of a whirlwind that she had never been to his home, and so she had no idea he was so obsessed with keeping old papers and stuff. She had assumed that his reluctance to show her his apartment before the wedding was just a "normal" bachelor's reluctance to reveal his lack of homemaking skills. How wrong she was! Her husband suffered from a serious mental illness, but she would never have guessed it unless she was in his home. Time would have let her discover this problem, but haste prevented it. Unfortunately for them, he refused to seek help and only grew more obsessed, until the home became a fire hazard. At that point she had to move out.

Take your time!

10. HAVE SEX ON THE FIRST DATE, OR ANY DATE, BEFORE THE WEDDING

Oh, boy, now we have gone and spoiled your fantasy. How old-fashioned can we be? Are we serious? After all, what if you and your boyfriend are not sexually compatible? What if you do not like the same things sexually? How can anyone not have sex, anyway? Nobody waits until marriage anymore—right?

There are a number of good reasons to forgo sex before marriage. Here are some of them.

Abstaining before marriage proves to you both that fidelity and monogamy are possible. If you are able to keep your physical urges in their proper place before marriage, you will be more able to trust each other to do so later. If he is willing to have sex before the wedding, who is to say he will not find a reason to have it with someone else after the wedding?

Abstaining before marriage elevates sexual intercourse to its rightful position as an outward symbol of an internal, spiritual, and emotional reality. When Moses described the creation of woman and man, he stated, "For this reason a man will leave his father and mother and be united to his wife, and they will become one flesh" (Gen. 2:24). God's intention of men and women leaving, cleaving, and then becoming one flesh was something Jesus affirmed as well. When the religious leaders of the day asked Him whether divorce was acceptable for any cause at all, Jesus answered by saying:

> Haven't you read . . . that at the beginning the Creator "made them male and female," and said, "For this reason a man will leave his father and mother be united to his wife, and the two will become one flesh"? So they are no longer two, but one. Therefore what God has joined together, let man not separate. (Matt. 19:4–6)

From creation, God ordained a certain order for the relationship between woman and man. Even the secular world used to recognize this fact with the old ditty: "First comes love, then comes marriage, then comes baby in a baby carriage." Leaving father and mother is significant. It represents maturity, being grown up enough to take care of oneself and one's progeny. According to God's design, "cleaving," or being united with another person, is to be a public, permanent commitment made before the whole community. Sexual intercourse is to be the culmination of leaving childhood behind and taking on new commitments and responsibilities, a unity of purpose symbolized by the act itself.

And in case you are wondering, marriage does make a difference. Sex is just sex outside of marriage. It may be fun, it may be risky, it may be enjoyable, but it is not the glorious unity of two souls that happens in marriage.

There is a mysterious change that occurs when two people are united in marriage, even if they are unbelievers. Countless couples can testify to the transformation that being married makes. Women and men were designed to be united in marriage. That is the best, the ideal, to which we can all aspire. Animals have sex. Humans marry.

Abstaining before marriage shows our willingness to place honor and nobility ahead of selfish pleasures. Our world is a hotbed of selfishness. "Me, myself, and I" is the theme of the millennium. My needs, my wants, and my passions are the only important ingredients in any relationship. But bringing these attitudes under the discipline of celibacy

before marriage strengthens our commitment to one another by prov-
ing we can rise above self-absorption. If he cannot put aside passion
and self-interest now, how will he do so later, when there are children
to consider?

*Abstaining before marriage protects the couple from sexually
transmitted diseases.* (This point assumes that both people are virgins
or have not been infected by previous sexual encounters.) While those
who have suffered from a sexually transmitted disease are able to enjoy
a happy, committed marriage and fulfilling physical relationship, not
having to deal with all that these diseases entail makes life a lot easier.

*Abstaining before marriage protects future children from the stigma
of illegitimacy.* While the stigma attached to out-of-wedlock birth is
almost a thing of the past, knowing that one's parents were committed
enough to make a family the right way provides a deep sense of security
to a child. Even when parents marry after discovering the pregnancy, the
child is left with the nagging doubt that he or she was the reason they
married. This doubt places a burden of guilt on the child that, although
not rational, can still feel all too real.

No child wants to feel he or she was a "mistake" or an after-
thought of a moment of careless passion. All children need the security of a home where both the man and woman are committed to each
other and to the integrity of family life. And being able to point to
their faithfulness and commitment before marriage gives parents a
great deal of credibility when their children become teens and wonder
about these issues.

WHAT TO DO IF YOU HAVE BLOWN IT

What if you have made one or more of these mistakes? Is there any
hope? Are you doomed to a succession of Mr. Wrongs, never to find
Mr. Right? Is there anything you can do to put yourself back on a

healthier path? Here are some tips to help you get moving in the right direction.

BE SURE TO FIND FORGIVENESS

Unresolved guilt is one of the most destructive forces, spiritually and psychologically, that we can face. When we blow it, we need forgiveness from God, from ourselves, and sometimes from others. Looking at ourselves honestly can be very painful, but it is worth the effort. We all have strengths and weaknesses. We all fail to live up to our own expectations, to say nothing of God's standards. The Bible says that if we confess our faults to one another, we are opening ourselves to healing from God (James 5:16). The old adage "Confession is good for the soul" is true even in this new millennium. Forgiveness releases power: God's power, the power to love and to change, and the power to forgive another person. Without forgiveness we become shriveled versions of ourselves, dried up and useless. Guilt poisons our souls in ways that are both subtle and obvious.

So if you have goofed, find forgiveness. Seek out a pastor or minister and start the process by talking. Be honest with yourself. If doing so would not hurt anyone else, find a way to make amends—to yourself and to others. And then let go of it. Go on. The Bible says: "If we confess our sins, he is faithful and just and will forgive us our sins and purify us from all unrighteousness" (1 John 1:9). Not only can God forgive, He can also cleanse us and heal the hurts that our mistakes and sins have left behind.

ADJUST YOUR EXPECTATIONS

Often our mistakes come about as a result of unrealistic expectations of either ourselves or others. Some of us expect too much of ourselves, some too little. Some expect too much of others and not enough of themselves. Whatever the reason, disappointment is the result.

If you have figured out that the man you thought was Mr. Right is really Mr. Wrong, hanging on to the relationship in hopes he will change is not realistic. Hanging on to save face and to spare yourself the heartache of a breakup is not worth it. Confront the *facts*. You will survive. Pain is pain, but it does pass. You can recover your peace and your dignity.

Do not give up and sink into despair. If you feel as if you are stuck and cannot move on without help, then *get help*. There is no shame in needing the support and guidance of others. We have all needed it at one time or another. Many fine Christian organizations and churches offer support, counseling, and other resources. If you feel trapped, reach out for the life preserver you need.

Change Your Behaviors

Once we get real about Mr. Wrong, it is crucial that we put the energy generated by our change in expectations to good use. It is *so* easy to fall back into old patterns of behavior. Change is uncomfortable, and the familiar is much less threatening than new, untried behaviors. Some of us thrive on change, but others shrink from it. Whatever our personality, we must decide to actually develop new behaviors rather than continue to do what does not work.

What kind of behaviors might have to change? Here are a couple you might find important.

First, change where you go and with whom you spend time. If your goal is to marry a person who does not abuse drugs or alcohol, but your favorite after-work hangout is a bar, you might have to go elsewhere. If your goal is to be treated with dignity and respect, but the only men you socialize with tend to be male chauvinists, you will need to reestablish your circle of friends. If your desire is to marry a college graduate, but the only people you know have all dropped out of high school, you will need to expand your exposure to more educated people.

Second, stop "hooking up" sexually and become celibate until you marry. Sleeping around only sets you up for heartache and pain, now and in the future. The need for sexual fulfillment, while wonderful and important in the marriage relationship, is *not* like the need to breathe, eat, or drink water. No one ever died from not having sex! (Unfortunately, many people have died from promiscuous behaviors that resulted in sexually transmitted diseases and damaging relationships.)

You can control your impulses. Your body and its urges do not have to dominate your life. Our society does not want to be disciplined in very many areas of life, especially sex. Those who wait to have sex until marriage are viewed as repressed, uneducated, or foolish. Yet what is repressed, uneducated, or foolish about deciding what you want and disciplining yourself and your urges to get it?

A good example of people who control their urges are athletes. You ask any serious athlete if she likes eating properly, working out, sweating like crazy, and pushing through pain to her physical goal. She will say that her urge to stop and give up is sometimes almost overwhelming. Yet she presses on, often against great odds. She sacrifices the pleasure of the moment for the delayed gratification of a goal later achieved. She fights her natural impulse to give in to fatigue, fear, anger, or some other human feeling. She perseveres because she knows how important it is to get to the goal. She is determined that nothing will hold her back.

All through human history there have been people who were willing to bring their bodies under discipline for a worthy goal. There have also always been those, who, like Esau in the Old Testament, sold their birthright for a pot of stew. We always have choices. If your goal is to repair the damage that has come to you through past promiscuity, then you will have to change your sexual behavior. You will have to learn to stop acting as if sex is the most important human urge.

If your goal is to eventually find a worthy man who will honor your commitment to remain celibate until marriage, you may have to learn to dress modestly (read that *modestly*, not *frumpily*), to stop teasing men sexually, to stop watching R-rated movies or reading trashy romance novels that stir your sexual urges. There are many actions that make up a celibate life, but they all start in the mind. If you do not decide to change, you will not change.

Develop New Skills

As we attempt to change old habits and develop new behaviors, success may seem slow in coming. We have the information about needing to change (knowledge), the proper expectations (attitude) about changing, and we are making changes (behavior), but we find we still are falling short. Why? It is probably as simple as this: we just need some skill enhancement. We need some hands-on training.

For example, Jane was a young woman who had led a pretty racy life until she encountered Jesus in a personal way in grad school. As she came to know Him, she began to desire to clean up her act. She longed to find a good Christian man who shared her enthusiasm for Jesus and who would respect her efforts to change her sexual behaviors. The problem was that ever since she was a preteen, Jane had always related to men in a sexual manner. This behavior began when her cousins molested her and she quickly learned to view sex as a "So what?" behavior. She had never had a male friend, only sex partners.

Jane knew all the buttons to push to get a guy going sexually. She did not even realize sometimes that she was doing this. Jane decided that she needed some new skills in her interpersonal repertoire. She began to notice how godly women at church (single and married) carried themselves, what language they used, how they dressed, and how they related to men as brothers, not sex objects. She asked an older woman in the church how to be friends with a man without sexualizing the relationship. Together they worked out a plan for Jane to use in assessing her own behaviors that tended to sexualize the relationships, and in practicing new, neutral, sisterly behaviors.

Jane also courageously went to one of the older men in the church with her mentor and asked him what behaviors men expect in a woman who is sexually pure. She asked questions she had never been able to ask before and became much more sensitive to how certain actions affect men in general, and what she could do instead. For example, clothes that are revealing suggest availability and destroy mystery. The woman who has a confident modesty combined with stylish clothes provides the right balance for a man who is interested in a woman with sexual integrity. She is not a prude, but she is also far from looking cheap, desperate, or seductive.

The bottom line is, you *can* change. If you have made any of the ten mistakes listed above, you can recover. You are not stuck with past failures. You can forgive and be forgiven. You can move on. It is up to you.

If you are still in search mode, be aware of mistakes you can make, and avoid them like the plague. Mr. Right may be just around the corner!

PART IV

WHEN THE SEARCH IS OVER

CHAPTER 14

ONCE YOU HAVE FOUND MR. RIGHT

What happens when you think you have found Mr. Right? If you and your guy are beginning to talk marriage, there are a few things you should ask yourself. Even the best-matched couple needs to examine their feelings and thoughts about the relationship before they say "I do." Without question, premarital counseling is the best divorce prophylactic. You may think you are too old, too experienced, or too spiritual to need premarital counseling. You may think that it is only for eighteen-year-olds who don't know anything about life. Guess again. You'd be surprised at how much benefit you can receive from a little prep work before marriage.

TEN QUESTIONS TO ASK YOURSELF

Why are these questions important? Because even if your man *is* Mr. Right, you are both still human beings and have a lot of differences in personality, culture, upbringing, likes, and dislikes. These questions,

along with premarital counseling, help identify a couple's future prob‐
lems and offer guidance for overcoming them. No one wants to get
married and encounter more strife than is normal or necessary.

They are also important because most engaged or nearly engaged
couples are so excited and full of bliss, they don't think about conflicts
to come. Often their goal is to put the best face on the relationship
rather than to focus on its potential or actual defects.

There is also a certain amount of social pressure to maintain the
relationship and see it through to the altar once its nature has been
displayed publicly. The couple's state of delight, combined with a need
to "look good," may keep them from facing honestly some of the nor‐
mal limitations in their relationship. Thus they may end up marrying
with unrealistic expectations.

When this happens, as the bliss fades and with it idealization, they
start to blame each other for not living up to expectations. This
blame/shame game leads inevitably to conflict. Such conflict can be
avoided, or at least reduced, if the couple is wise enough before mar‐
riage to examine their relationship and expectations honestly. Questions
such as these are useful for beginning such a dialogue.

We suggest asking yourself these questions and asking your
intended to answer them for himself as well. Better yet, answer the
questions with the pastor who is going to marry you or with a trained
professional counselor. He or she can help you sort out how to best
resolve your problems and how to strategize for further growth once
you are married.

1. What I appreciate the most about my beloved is _____.

2. What I dislike the most about my beloved is _____.

3. The biggest change or adjustment I will have to make once
   we are married will be _____.

4. What concerns me the most about marrying this person is
_____.

5. When I marry, the biggest change or adjustment I anticipate
with my family of origin is _____.

6. The thing that makes me the angriest is _____.

7. Of my family, my beloved is closest to _____.

8. Of my family, my beloved is least close to _____.

9. _____ is the most difficult subject for us to talk about.

10. Our greatest asset or strength is _____.

RATING YOURSELF; RATING HIM

Here is a little quiz. On a scale of 1–10, rate yourself and then your
partner (1 = Rarely or not at all; 10 = Always).

1. Imperfect: has weaknesses; has annoying faults.

2. Responsible: blames no one else for problems, makes most
of talents, opportunities.

3. Patient: can wait for sex or for something not in the budget,
is able to restrain self from saying mean-spirited things.

4. Communicative: able to share deepest feelings and thoughts,
interests, goals, differences.

5. Friendly: open, warm, has deep relationships outside of
yours, treats others with respect.

6. Purposeful: has values and aspirations loftier than a big
bank account or material possessions.

7. Spiritual: demonstrates a genuine walk with God and has a vibrant faith that makes a difference in everyday living.

8. Childproof: likes kids, feels at ease with them, does not need to compete with them for love, does not think they are inconvenient.

9. Trustworthy: tells the truth, lives honorably, does the right thing even if it is not popular.

10. Loving: knows the beloved well and how to be a good lover and friend to him or her, demonstrates "tough love" when necessary, builds up others.

SCORING:

1–10:   You and/or your intended need to get some help right now!

11–20: You may need to rethink your readiness for marriage.

21–30: You still have some growing up to do! A mentor or counselor would help.

31–40: You are in need of some personal growth and encouragement. Get some feedback from a trusted pastor, parent, friend, or mentor.

41–50: You are on the edge. Get some help in your personal development to speed you toward your goals.

51–60: You are on the upswing. Pick out the areas you need to keep working on.

61–70: You are doing better than most but still can improve. Keep going!

71–80:   You are well prepared to be someone's Mr. or Ms. Right. You have faults but are actively working on them.

81–90:   You are a super candidate! Keep up the good work!

91–100: You are either in denial or you deserve an Academy Award! *Nobody* is this good.

Committing to another person in marriage is a huge step. Being prepared by honestly assessing your strengths and weaknesses is a crucial part of maturely approaching marriage. It is much easier to break an engagement than to get a divorce.

We are amazed at the number of couples who come for counseling and say, "Oh, we never talked about *that*" or "Oh, we just assumed we'd figure it out" or "We never thought that would matter because we were so in love." Love is grand, but it is also blind. Good marriages come from going into the commitment with your eyes wide open and your expectations realistic.

CHAPTER 15

HOW TO DESTROY MR. RIGHT AND YOUR CHANCE TO BE WITH HIM

Have you ever known someone who had a wonderful husband, yet ended up ruining him or, more accurately, the relationship? You know what we mean: he was a good man, but she expected him to be perfect. Or he was quiet, and she expected him to be an extrovert. Or he earned a good middle-class income, but she nagged him into taking a job he hated for more money.

It seems as if some people are never satisfied, and never happy. No matter what you do, they always find something to criticize. And when you complain, they justify their griping as being "for your own good." They are the kind of people who ruin marriages. They produce dispirited children. They discourage even the most optimistic among us. They may have found a Mr. Right to start with, but along the way they destroyed him in one way or another.

HOW TO RUIN MR. RIGHT

No one wants to ruin a potentially good relationship, but it does happen. What are the ways you could destroy your relationship with Mr. Right?

1. Expect Him to Be Perfect

He may be right for you, but he will never be perfect. No one can be wonderful in all areas, at all times. We like to think that at least we ourselves are almost perfect, but the honest approach forces us to face reality. We are all flawed at the core by sin, and no matter how good we look on the outside, we all have our weaknesses, foibles, and haunting habits. None of us would have a leg to stand on compared to God's glory without His grace. We may think we are right, wise, or more mature than the next person, but compared to God we are empty, foolish, and prone to error.

This fact does not make us worthless, however; it gives us a basis from which to be humble every day. Your Mr. Right may be just right for you, but he will never be perfect, and neither will you! The dangerous thing about being a perfectionist is that you may be living in perfect denial. Ask friends and family if your standards are beyond anything anyone could reach.

2. Spoil Him by Being a Doormat

Giving a man everything his heart desires can quickly turn Mr. Right into Mr. Brat. Waiting on him as if he is helpless does not engender respect for you in his mind. If anything, it shows him how little self-respect you actually have. I will never forget hearing about an elderly couple who had been married for sixty years. Retired and living in a nice retirement community, they enjoyed having one or two other couples from their complex in for lunch once in a while. One time, the wife made chicken sandwiches for everyone, set them on plates, and passed them on to each person. They prayed over the food, and as everyone else began to eat, her husband looked up with a doleful expression and said softly, "Mine's not cut." His wife got up and went over and cut it for him. The other couples just looked on in amazement. The wife had lived with his dependent behavior for so long that she never gave it a second thought.

Another example was a man and woman who had been married about thirty-five years. Their daughter told me that for as long as she could remember, her dad had gone in every night and sat on the edge of the bed, and her mom came in, knelt down, and removed his shoes and socks. This act of servanthood was not instituted because her dad was disabled or too frail to do it himself. He just expected it. Her mom dutifully did it until the day he died.

Some women have the mistaken idea that if they are a "good" wives, they always do everything their husbands ask, demand, or want. They think that being submissive means being subservient. They often cite the Ephesians 5 passage about submission of wives to the husband, but do not include the rest of the passage that talks about mutual submission of the woman and the man to God and to one another.

In the excellent book *10 Lies the Church Tells Women* (Creation House, 2000), J. Lee Grady outlines why so many Christian women suffer in abusive marriages and their church leaders do not help them. He encourages all women to pursue God and fulfill their divine destiny. No man truly respects a woman who is a wimp. He may take advantage of her, use her, and abuse her, but he will not respect her.

3. REJECT HIM WHEN HE DOES NOT MEASURE UP TO DEAR OL' DAD

Some women had wonderful dads. They were blessed with fathers who loved their moms and were good with the kids. These women flourished under their dads' guidance and love, learning to like themselves because they were loved so well. Even when they were at the "ugly duckling" stage in junior high, their dads still somehow made them feel special and even pretty. Some dads were warm and affectionate, some were quiet and steady, some were extroverted and cheerful, but they all communicated well with their daughters in one way or another.

These daughters glowed with pride when they pleased Dad, and wilted like flowers in the hot August sun when they disappointed them. They admired, adored, and wanted to be like their fathers. And they certainly wanted their husbands to have all of those good traits. What would be wrong with that, since Dad was such a good man?

Well, in many ways there is nothing wrong with wanting a good man like Dad. Certainly it is a blessing to have had a dad who modeled what a man should be. Sometimes to a new husband, however, a great father-in-law becomes a threat. Mr. Right begins to think that he will never measure up to his wife's standard. And even if he is a generally good man himself, he may come to feel he is in competition for your love and admiration.

While your Mr. Right probably has some of the great character points your dad had, he still will never be your dad. He will never understand you or put up with you in the same ways Dad does. He may not laugh at your jokes or compliment you in the same gentle way your papa did. He may be an extrovert, not the quiet introvert your father was. He may earn more money or be more generous—or more stingy—than your dad. He may pay the bills on time or not. He may drink an occasional beer or not. He may be fervent and outspoken with his beliefs, or not.

No matter how much Dad and your husband have in common, they are not clones. You must allow for differences, or your new Mr. Right will start to resent the comparison.

4. COMPARE HIM TO OTHER MEN

You meet women who make this type of comparison all the time. You see them on television. You hear them at the social events griping about their inadequate husbands. No matter what the husband's successes, there is always some area where he does not measure up to Fred from high school or Marty from college or Rose's husband, Jack. *All the other dads help their kids with homework and do the dishes after dinner,* she thinks. Or *Jill's husband never yells at her.* Or *My first husband really knew how to barbecue, unlike Sam here.* Or *Susie's husband joined the fathers' ministry at church—why can't he?*

All this criticism is wearing. It eats away at a man's self-esteem. It gnaws at him like cancer. Probably the most destructive behaviors a wife can use to destroy a relationship are criticism and comparison to other men. And these things have turned many Mr. Rights into bitter, deflated, defeated, and angry shades of their former selves.

When we measure ourselves against anyone else, we shortchange everyone. No man wants to be measured by someone else's success, personality, appearance, or spiritual gifts. Men (and women) want to be appreciated for who they are, not for how much they are like some other person.

Men resent comparison. They want to be your one and only, your hero. They do not need to know that "So-and-So can do it better." Believe me! One of the biggest complaints we hear in marital counseling is, "Nothing I do for her is good enough. She is never pleased."

5. ALWAYS AGREE WITH HIM

Even Mr. Right has an ego, and flattery and manipulation will ruin even the best of men. Withholding genuine feedback because he might be hurt or angry is not helpful. Any counselor can tell you of couples who come for help, and the husband's statement is something like: "She never told me she did not like that. How was I to know? I cannot read her mind!" Or "She always said she *liked* that. I did not know she was faking it." We all need to hear the truth, gently and lovingly expressed. Never disagreeing with your man, or never telling him what you really need or feel, may keep the peace temporarily, but it may also spoil him rotten or lead to great disillusionment and despair once the truth comes out. (And trust us, it will!)

Some women take the idea of not criticizing their husbands to an extreme. They think any feedback is criticism. Opinions, information, feelings are not criticism. You can give them in a demeaning or critical manner, or you can share them in a respectful and compassionate manner. Think about it. If you know someone loves you deeply and wants to improve your relationship with him, and he tells you—sensitively and clearly—something you are doing wrong, do you not receive it better from him than from someone else? Why? Because you trust him to have your best interest at heart. You do not hear what he says as criticism because you know in your heart that he loves you.

Well, Mr. Right is no different. Do not withhold your feedback, wisdom, experience, or point of view from the man you love. He may not always admit it, but he needs it as much as he needs anything else you can give him.

6. You Nag Him

Nagging and browbeating do not make for a successful relationship. These tactics lead only to resentment and anger for both parties. It is especially easy to fall into this pattern with a man who is by personality more passive than you are. Those of us who are "go-getters" tend to think everyone else in the universe should be the way we are! We want things done quickly, or even without our asking, and done correctly the first time. Do you recognize yourself? Well, be careful, for you are a potential nag.

Yipes! Who wants to be a nag? What in the world can you do

instead? Setting boundaries and consequences are alternatives to nagging that make much more sense. People are a lot like dogs: they respond well to praise and need immediate results. When training a puppy and reinforcing a behavior, what do you do? You praise it wildly and give a treat instantly upon its accomplishment. You do not stand there and say nothing, nor do you yell at the puppy for not doing it quickly enough. Positive reinforcement always works better than punishment. Living with someone who is more passive than you are can be a challenge (but it is no picnic for him living with you either, Ms. Go-Getter).

If he never gets around to some things around the house or in your relationship, accept it and move on. Do it yourself (send yourself the flowers), hire someone else to do it, or just forget it.

There are few things in life that are worth nagging a man to death over. Let him know your boundary. For example: "If you cannot get to the leaves by Friday, I am paying the neighbor kid twenty bucks to do it." Then follow through. Threats are just another form of nagging.

7. SMOTHER AND WORSHIP HIM

While everyone wants to be admired, and we all need affirmation and attention, no one likes to be smothered and idolized. Being put on a pedestal can be very shame inducing to a man because he *knows* he is not that perfect. Knowing that he can never live up to the high expectations of the woman who adores him creates a sense of inadequacy and even shame. He wants to live up to the idealized self the woman sees, but knows he cannot, because he is only human. Sometimes this shame and double-bind feeling leads a man to just give up. He thinks: "Well, I'll never be what she thinks I am, so I am messed up already. When she discovers that I am not perfect, she will reject me. So I might as well fail now and get it over with."

Another problem with idealizing your mate is that it makes the relationship inherently unequal. You are automatically one-down. After a while all that looking up is apt to give you a crick in your neck! The easiest way to start resenting your husband is to think he is perfect. You have gifts and talents just as your Mr. Right does. By focusing so adoringly on his gifts or talents, you neglect your own. We are called to love others "as we love ourselves," and if we are so enamored of the other we cannot properly assess our own contributions and gifts in life.

Many women focus on their Mr. Right and his good qualities because they unconsciously think they do not deserve him. They end up smothering him with adoration and attention, thinking they are being loving. No man wants a leech or a groupie for a wife. If this is your tendency, you better get a life before you tie the knot with Mr. Right, or you are headed for problems.

8. You Tell Him What to Do

Despite the television show *Yes, Dear. . .* having a bossy wife is no picnic. Just as nagging is a pain, so is being bossy or know it all. Children need instruction. Most adults, unless mentally disabled, do not. If your husband wants to be ordered around, he can join the armed services. He does not need a sergeant at home! You don't like being ordered about like a slave or a soldier, so why should he?

It is one thing if your husband asks you how to do something. It is altogether another if you take it upon yourself to tell him. Think about how annoying it is to drive with a backseat driver. You get so you want to reach back and smack the person, right? If you want your husband to resent and disrespect you, keep telling him how to do things. So he doesn't fold the towels the way you do it. So what? So he uses the dust buster to vacuum the throw rugs. Who cares? In one hundred years it will not matter much, will it? If it inconveniences you horridly, ask if you can show him how you prefer it, while admitting to being "too picky" or "a bit fussy." Explain why you like it the way you do, and then if he remembers to do it that way, great. If not, forget it. It is not worth the energy! Also, do not try to tell him how to organize and run an area of *his* responsibility. It is one thing if the kitchen (for example) is your domain and you ask him to do something your way, but it is all together a cow of a different color if you interfere in his domain. You would not put up with him telling you how to sew or drive your car, so why should he put up with your telling him how to drive his car, rake the lawn, or fold his own laundry?

9. YOU NEVER HOLD HIM ACCOUNTABLE

Of course, you may be one of those women who never holds herself accountable for anything either! But assuming that is not true, ask yourself if you want to spend the rest of your life with someone who always gets his way, and is never accountable to keep his promises, do his work, carry his load or to act responsibly in the relationship? Accountability is what makes relationships work. If it is all about *me*, and I can do whatever I want, and you will always put up with me and my antics, why should I care about *you*? I can walk on you, stomp on our vows, disregard your welfare, and still expect you to hang on like a devoted puppy dog. Most people understand that if you love your kids, you hold them to a certain, sure, and steady standard. You are not authoritarian or mean or cruel: you are firm in holding them to reasonable expectations. Why? Because you love them and want them to learn to be well-socialized and able to function in society. You want them to have an understanding of consequences.

Men do not respect women who put up with anything and everything. So why do some men get away with bad behavior? Because women put up with it. As women, we tend to be afraid that the man will leave us or reject us if we hold him accountable to be noble or strong or truthful. The reality is that if he is Mr. Right, he will want you to hold him accountable. He will want your input when it is given in a loving, constructive manner. At times all of us are tempted to live down to our lowest nature, rather than aspire to the best and the better. We all need women and men who will hold us accountable to aim for the goal of our highest calling in Christ Jesus, as members of God's household.

10. You Withhold Sex When He Does Not Act Like You Want Him To Act

Sex is not a tool or a toy to be used to manipulate or punish your man. Yet that is the message the media gives young women today. *Tease him, flirt outrageously, and then pull back and taunt him. Dangle the carrot but never deliver.* Instead of encouraging modesty and chastity, our culture and its icons in the media encourage flaunting your body parts, dressing provocatively, and then being outraged when a man wants to touch you. If this is the message you are sending before marriage, it can only lead to continued manipulation after the wedding. If you tease him now, and use sex to get what you want before the vows are taken, what makes you think it will be any different later?

One woman said in counseling, that after fifteen years of marriage she is just now realizing that even after becoming a Christian, she used sex to manipulate her boyfriend (later husband), and continued it into the marriage. When he was disparaging of her or critical of her appearance or critiqued her housekeeping skills, she conveniently decided to "have a headache" or just pretend to be asleep that evening. She realized her weight gain after the four kids was not all related to the pregnancies and that she was using it to make her husband angry, since he had been so unsupportive as a dad to their kids. She knew her weight bugged him; so she unconsciously at first kept the extra fat on to annoy him. Now that she is aware of this manipulation within her, she is seeking to submit herself to the Lord and go to her therapist for accountability not to use sex or her appearance as a weapon against her husband.

Sex is a God-given joy in the context of a loving, committed marriage. It is not to be squandered for our personal power over someone else. The Bible does allow for couples to mutually agree to stop having marital relations for a brief time for a time of prayer and seeking the Lord (I Cor. 7: 1-5). However, to just withhold sex from one another to manipulate or punish each other is not loving. The exception, of course, is when there is genuine abuse in the relationship. When there is abuse, adultery, or addiction in a relationship, part of holding a spouse accountable may be separating and not being sexual with that person for a time. A Christian counselor who is trained in marriage counseling can give a couple guidelines to evaluate their relationship sexually to see if it is healthy or based on manipulation. (By the way, we have seen in our practices just as many men as women complain about their spouses withholding sex from them. This complaint from women has risen dramatically with the introduction of internet porn into our society.)

11. When Kids Come Along, You Get Preoccupied and/or Obsessed with Them and Neglect Him

Young mothers complain that all they hear all day is baby talk. Young dads complain all they hear is "I'm too tired." Anyone who has been around babies and youngsters for any length of time knows that they are a twenty-four hour, seven-day-a-week challenge. It is easy for a young wife and mother to become so focused on her new responsibilities as a parent, that she forgets to nurture herself and her husband. Why is the Dead Sea dead? Because it has no outlet. Any body of water that is not giving and receiving will eventually become stagnant. Many young moms feel so responsible that they forget to exercise, pray, relax, or keep up with friends. They do so much for everyone else, that there is nothing left over to give to the husband, much less to herself. Years ago when grandparents, cousins, aunts, and uncles live with the rural family from time to time, young women had a break. They could go outside and garden or work in the barn or with the animals. They would go pick blueberries and have a couple hours to think and pray. They had someone else who would watch the kids for a while so they could quilt or sew or make apple butter. They could chat with neighbors at a picnic or a barn raising or a church social. Today life is so hurried, and so full of activities that are individually focused, there is precious little time to reflect, pray, or chat. Without these elements of balance, any Jane will become a Plain Dull Jane in no time. Young moms are often isolated and alone, and think (rightly or wrongly) that no one, including their husbands, understands how hard they work. When he comes home and wants attention too, it all becomes too much. Feelings of depression, inadequacy, self-doubt or even self-hate begin to creep in and damage the marital relationship.

In other cases, the wife as new mom finds a magical new identity. Suddenly she has purpose, meaning, and fulfillment in her life. She throws her whole self into this parenting process, and forgets all about being a wife. The children come first, and husband is a distant second, or third, after the dog. After all, he is an adult and can fend for himself, can't he? Being a *mom* becomes the source of the woman's self esteem, and she is reluctant to step back and see herself as "just a wife." The children *need* her after all, and how could she ever leave them to go out on a date night or away for the weekend with her husband. Why how selfish can he be? This type of scenario is ripe for turning your Mr. Right into Mr. Philanderer. He may find his needs met by someone who will give him the attention and affirmation he used to get from you. Your calling as a wife is to God first, husband second, and kids third. When kids see that Mom and Dad put each other first, after the Lord, they feel secure and safe. When one parent focuses unduly on the children it unbalances the family system and someone gets left out. You can love your kids, but remember to love your husband first.

12. You Cease to Grow and Change with Him

Life goes on. Things and the universe change whether we want it to do so or not. We are not able to hold on to high school memories or college chums. We age, our cars age, and even our parents age. New responsibilities come. Old ones fade away. Each stage of life presents new challenges, and if we do not grow and change with each new stage, we are left behind wondering what happened.

Adapting to change and growing do not mean abandoning our Christian values or chosen ideals. It does mean adjusting to the changing realities around us. I can remember when microwaves first came onto the American scene. I scoffed and said, "I would *never* need one of those things." Guess who cannot imagine cooking without one now? Same with computers, cell phones, pagers, etc.

If I stick to my own familiar ways of doing things, I will be left behind. If my spouse is growing spiritually and emotionally, but I resist and refuse to look at myself and my own needs, I will get left behind. If my husband and children develop hobbies and share activities, and I sit at home alone and refuse to learn how to join in, I will be boring, dull, and left out. If I hang on to my outmoded, childish ways of dealing with stress, anger, fears, and frustrations that life throws in my path, I will be lonely and alienated and wonder why no one wants to be around me.

Change is threatening, hard, and wondrous if you give it a try. Jesus has promised that He never changes and will always be with us (Matt. 28: 20). Our security comes not from hanging on to the past and our old defense mechanisms and habits of thinking, but from Him. He has a plan that is for our welfare (Jer. 29:11), and while it will involve change and dying to self (Col. 3: 1–17; Matt. 8: 19–22), He is with us all the way, guiding and leading us to become more like Himself (2 Cor. 3: 18). Don't get stuck with being who you are now. Ask God to show you where you need to change and grow, and then begin the adventure with Him at your side!

13. You Always Expect Him to Make More Money This Year Than Last Year

Boy, does this one irk men or what? The last thing a guy wants is to be thought of as just a paycheck. Some women complain that "men just think of women as sex objects," but men have a valid complaint about some women as well. Many women today are self-supporting and contribute equally or more to the family finances. Yet there are some women who are still acting like gold-diggers. Men are the eternal source of greenbacks, and if they fail to ante up, heaven help them!

In our materialistic society, it is easy for women and men to become enamored of things, things, and more things. A bigger house, a nicer car, a new SUV, a cottage for the weekends. Competing with neighbors, or worse, with siblings to see who is more successful financially can put a lot of pressure on a man if he is the sole breadwinner. Few women who have not been sole breadwinners understand the enormous emotional burden it is for a man to get up every day and know that his family's food, shelter and life depends on what he can bring in. Granted, as a Christian man he should, and probably is, trusting God to provide, but he is still the one who has to get up every day, get on the bus, and greet the boss. God is faithful, but manna stopped flowing from heaven quite some time ago. Last time I looked, most people have to work for their daily bread.

Expecting a man to earn more and more and more is not fair. Everyone has an earning potential, but no one's potential is unlimited. While some men are indeed lazy, if this one is your Mr. Right, we can safely assume that laziness is not one of his character traits. As believers, we are exhorted to learn, as Paul the Apostle did, to be content in all circumstances (Phil. 4: 10–13). Remember, the wedding vows say "for richer, for poorer." Nothing spoils a good romance quicker than a greedy wife.

14. YOU LAUGH AT HIM WHEN HE IS WEAK OR VULNERABLE

Kicking a guy when he is down is one sure way to ruin the relationship! When the Bible tells us to "submit to one another" (Eph. 5:21) the word *submit* means to come underneath and support or lift up. Tearing someone down with ridicule or sarcasm is the height of immaturity and mean-spiritedness. As marriage partners, both women and men are to come underneath and support one another, in times of strength and weakness. Part of the reason people seek to be married is to have support and help when things get tough. Having his wife laugh at him when he has made a mistake, or when he is vulnerable in some way, is devastating to a husband. Telling him he is "being silly" or "stupid" when he shares a deep feeling or concern with you will only push him away from you. Shaming someone when they fail is a sure way to keep them in the one-down position. It may give you a momentary power boost, but if equality and partnership is your goal in marriage, you are heading the wrong way when you laugh at your spouse.

15. YOU FORGET TO PRAY FOR HIM EVERY DAY

Life is hectic, and sometimes we forget to pray even for those who are most important to us. Prayer does change things. It changes us, and it changes the one pray for. We may not see it immediately, but that spiritual principle always works. When we seek God about something, we will find Him. We may not always get what we ask, but we will find Him. He is the answer we need, and the answer our husbands need. Every man needs a woman who will faithfully lift him up to God in prayer. Even a man who ridicules it needs it. Even a man who is wandering away from God needs it. Even a man who is growing spiritually needs it.

Keeping your eyes on God, and not on your man, will make you more generous with praise and less generous with criticism. Letting go and letting God handle him will reduce your anxiety and the urge to control, manipulate, or fix him. (He'll certainly like that!) Focusing on God as your source rather than manipulation and nagging always brings peace instead of chaos. So it is good for you, and it is good for him. When women pray, good things happen. More powerful changes in the world have been wrought by women who prayed than anyone will ever know here on earth. Just ask any mother!!

CHAPTER 16

TWELVE WAYS TO MAKE MR. RIGHT EVEN BETTER

Two heads are better than one when it comes to building character and personal strength. You won't be marrying Mr. Perfect, but you can help the man you love get as close as possible. You can hurt or you can help, and we have provided some ways to help.

TWELVE TOOLS FOR HOME IMPROVEMENT

1. APPRECIATE HIM

We all perform better when we feel appreciated. Some men are used to being nagged by their mothers and look for a wife to be an affirmer. When we are dating someone, it is easy to compliment, affirm, and support. After marriage the realities of everyday life set in and nagging becomes an easy habit. Men do not want to have an intimate relationship with someone who acts like Mom if Mom was a nagger. Many women think that being a wife is the same as being a mother—they are *supposed* to cajole, nag, coax, and yell to get things done. Then they wonder why their men act like children.

The urge to nag is connected to a lack of respect. If I respect you as another adult, I am not going to treat you as if you are only five years old. Mr. Right wants a woman who can negotiate and be flexible with her goals, and who can appreciate, affirm, and adapt by taking his goals into account. No one likes to feel controlled or ordered around.

Ms. Right does not capitulate and cave in to all his whims and desires, however. The heart of a good team is the ability to recognize what is needed from all sides and to give each side the respect it deserves. If all a woman sees is her own point of view, and she cannot affirm, understand, or uplift her husband's goals, the relationship is in trouble.

2. Accept Him as He Is

Too many women enter relationships thinking (at least subconsciously) that "with enough love" they can change their man into something else. They tend to ignore his weaknesses while dating, believing that with marriage and responsibility he will "grow." After the wedding, they may not harp and nag, but they put emotional pressure on him so that he knows he is not measuring up. He always feels under the gun, deficient, inadequate, and unsupported.

Accepting a spouse's personality, temperament, habits, likes, and dislikes is a huge part of marriage. If I keep ignoring the areas in which we are different, in hopes that they will go away, I will be rudely surprised one day when reality comes crashing in. Obviously it is easier to accept a person's strengths, especially if they complement my weak areas, than it is to accept his defects. But let's be clear: acceptance does not mean we never mention things that annoy us or cause true disruption to our relationship. It does mean we recognize that changes will occur only if the other person is willing. It is much wiser to go into a relationship facing the facts than to just hope he will change later.

If you do not like his spendthrift ways now, do not assume that he will change. Accept that if you marry him, you will probably need to work outside the home to supplement the family income. Then when you have to do so, you will not resent it. If you think he is too tied to his mother while you are dating, accept that when you are married she will probably be a frequent guest. That way, when he wants to have Mom move in with you, it will not be a shock.

If you hate dogs but insist on marrying a dog breeder, you are the one who will have to adjust. If he is in medical school when you meet, chances are he will be a doctor later! It will not be fair to act wounded and surprised that he keeps doctor's hours once you are married.

3. SERVE INSTEAD OF COMPETE

While it is easier to accept someone's strengths when they complement our weaknesses, how does it work if we both are strong in the same areas? How can you accept someone else's strength without competing with him? Too many modern marriages are like reality TV: contestants trying to best each other for the prize. It matters not if the prize is Best Parent or Sexiest Lover or Best Income Producer, the battle to win becomes the focus of the relationship. Rather than a partnership, the two individuals focus on outdoing each other in the various arenas of marriage and family life.

All of us have a certain amount of ego, and we *like* being better at things than someone else is. You may protest and say, "Oh, no. I am a shy, humble person. I hate the limelight. I am not a bit competitive." Yet have you ever listed for anyone all the sacrifices you have made to make your boyfriend, friend, husband, or child what he is today? Admit it: you enjoy feeling unappreciated because it lets you win the prize of Most Unrecognized!

So how do we balance our mutual strengths in a relationship? What if you both are good at balancing the checkbook? What if you both are gourmet cooks, great soloists, or first-rate skiers? What enables you to give up competing and enjoy each other?

The New Testament book of John gives us a clue in the story of Jesus washing the disciples' feet. In that culture and climate, people wore sandals, and the roads were dusty and hot. Washing feet was the job of the lowliest servant or slave in the household. As a host, if you did not offer foot-washing, you were considered very rude.

In John's account, Jesus and His followers had gathered to eat. They had arranged to have the Passover meal, a Jewish custom, catered. All the necessary items were provided for them, including a bowl, a pitcher, and a towel. One problem: no servant was there to do the dirty work. The disciples must have decided to ignore the issue of foot-washing before dinner and just gone ahead with the evening meal. But Jesus did not.

> Jesus knew that the Father had put all things under his power, and that he had come from God and was returning to God; so he got up from the meal, took off his outer clothing, and wrapped a towel around his waist. After that, he poured water into a basin and began to wash his disciples' feet, drying them with the towel that was wrapped around him. (John 13:3–5)

Here was Jesus the Messiah, the disciples' teacher and leader, and He was washing their feet. Even Peter had enough shame to protest, but Jesus insisted. How could Jesus humble Himself to such a level? Why, He was the Master! They should be washing His feet! The reason Jesus was able to perform this lowly task was because He decided to serve rather than compete with His followers. The apostle Paul described the proper attitude this way:

Do nothing out of selfish ambition or vain conceit, but in humility consider others better than yourselves. Each of you should look not only to your own interests, but also to the interests of others.

Your attitude should be the same as that of Christ Jesus:

> Who, being in very nature God,
>> did not consider equality with God
> something to be grasped [held onto],
>> but made himself nothing,
> taking the very nature of a servant,
>> being made in human likeness.

And being found in appearance as a man, he humbled himself and became obedient to death—even death on a cross! (Phil. 2:3–8)

How do we stop competing with each other's strengths? We voluntarily decide to be servants. We willingly give up our rights to be better or best and choose to serve our spouse, our family, our community. We can do this only if we follow Jesus' model: we need to know who we are in God's plan, where we come from, and where we are going. We need to understand that if we are going to follow Jesus' example, we will serve, not compete.

4. UNDERSTAND HIS ATTITUDE TOWARD SUCCESS

Each cultural group, each family, each man has his own definition of "success," but few women understand the tremendous emotional pressure men feel not to fail. And more men than you can imagine feel like total failures.

Men are very competitive. Men take the idea of dominion further than God intended, and so compete with each other, with nature, with the animal kingdom, with women, and with themselves. Their goal in

life is to *win,* whatever that means. Women are more interested in relationships, cooperation, teamwork, and harmony. Not men. They are
eager to enter the fray. They long to conquer *something,* anything.
They must achieve, dominate, fulfill their destiny.

Failure, then, is so shameful as to be unmentionable, if not unthink-
able. It is not that men are more vain or proud than women are, it is
just that the prize, the score, the win seems so much more important to
them in terms of their self-esteem. Women want to be successful but do
not define it in the same way men do. Even if they succeed in the competitive world of work or academia, often it is in their relationships
that women establish their sense of self. Outward achievements are
great, but relationships are forever, from a woman's point of view.

Men are pretty hard on themselves for any real or perceived failures.
No one comes out on top all of the time, and success in one area may
actually preclude success in another. Yet a man may feel that he should
be the best at everything, in all situations. Men often bear the role of
"answer person" or Mr. Fix It. So they assume that others expect them
always to be able to handle whatever comes. If a man's wife does not
understand how important it is to him to feel like a winner, she will inadvertently deprive him of support and affirmation when he needs it most.

Women have a great opportunity to help men remember that
healthy relationships can bring a type of success and self-esteem that
cannot be measured in terms of money, power, or status. The trust in
a child's eye, the pride on the face of one's parents—these are all successes women can encourage their men toward achieving.

5. HELP HIM RELATE TO YOU AS A WOMAN

Men assume that what works with other men will also work with
a wife and kids. Wrong! But they do not usually realize this fact without help from the women who love them. For example, guys kid each
other to show affection. If one sees an old friend after a long absence,

he might say something like, "Hey bud, you have gotten a little shiny on top there since the last time I saw you!" Both men will laugh, punch each other, and feel closer as a result. Ever notice how women and children often react to teasing? By taking the comments personally and becoming offended: "How could you say that?"

Another example: men take a mechanical approach to problems. They want to solve them. This is what they are rewarded for at work—their objectivity and direct approach. At home, however, jumping to solve the problem without showing empathy and listening to the feelings involved rarely goes well. Women and children like to have their emotions acknowledged and validated before someone tackles the problem. "All you care about is fixing things. You do not care how I feel!" is the lament of many a wife or teenager.

Lots of good men are totally unaware that they are using male bonding and relationship techniques with the wife and kids. And they are clueless as to why their sincere efforts are not working. Women can offer input and feedback to men about the difference between what works at home and what works in the male culture. They can assume that their men are sincere but misguided, not intentionally hurtful. Men need this feedback, not recrimination and blame.

6. Help Him to Have Fun

Life is so serious. Work, work, work, plan, plan, plan, strive, strive, strive. The opportunity to not take oneself so seriously does not come often. Routine dominates. Boredom stupefies. Surprise is rare, unless each person brings some lightheartedness and fun into the relationship.

Some men find it difficult to relax and let go. They need a woman to tickle their fancy, jiggle their funny bone, and jump-start their hilarity battery. Underneath every adult is a child who never got to have as much fun as he needed. You can encourage your man by helping him reconnect with that lovable little boy who has been hiding behind the *Wall Street Journal.*

Laughter really is good medicine. All of us live with so much stress that even a little chuckle can be a lifesaver. Your love and acceptance can be just the things your man needs to be able to relax and to find more joy in life.

7. HELP BALANCE HIS WEAKNESSES WITH YOUR STRENGTHS

In any good partnership, each person is able to use his or her strengths to balance the other person's weak points. No one is successful, gifted, or talented at everything. The Bible describes the church community as being like a physical body; that is, there are many parts, each with a different talent, but all work together for the same goal. Some parts are more noticeable, more glamorous, but all are necessary for the optimum function of the body (1 Cor. 12).

In the same way, God has gifted the human community with varying talents, skills, and preferences. God did not create us to be clones of one another. No one is totally self-sufficient. We all need other people in some way. You may be different from me but you bring to the world something I never could. I may be similar to you in some ways, but I am uniquely and wonderfully made. I offer my strengths to balance your weaknesses. You offer your strengths to balance mine.

How can you use this truth to encourage your man? Well, rather than harping on how much better your way is, or how defective his way is, you could focus on understanding the interplay between your strengths and weaknesses. You might be surprised to find that you complement each other more than you imagined. Use your strengths to refresh, build up, inspire, or challenge him. Let him use his strengths to balance out your weaker areas. If his strength is connecting with others and finding ways to enjoy others at sports events and recreational times, allow that strength in him to stretch you a bit and provide you with opportunities you would have never taken for yourself. If you tend to be kind of hyper and he is more calm, let him be the one to set the tempo in a crisis. Or if you are a bit of a spendthrift and he has good money skills, let him manage the money.

We all are needed, and we like to feel that way as well. If you flaunt your strengths to show him how much more competent, savvy, or gifted you are, you will find he begins to avoid you. If you seek ways to be supportive, to come alongside, to lift him up to greater achievements by using your strengths for his benefit, you will be surprised what happens in your relationship as a result.

8. Do Not Make Him Read Your Mind

Men are not mind readers any more than women are. Yet sometimes women seem to expect men to just "know" what they need, especially if they have been together for a long time. How many times we have heard in a counseling session, "Well, if he does not know by now, I am not going to tell him!" The reality is that unless women communicate clearly what they need and feel and think, men are left guessing.

Yes, it would be nice if he could just spontaneously intuit whatever you need from him, whenever you want it. But most do better with honest, up-front information. Just assuming that you have already communicated or that he understands without actual discussion will lead only to disappointment.

This is especially true of parenting issues. Little girls watch their moms and grandmothers nurture babies and young children. They mimic the behaviors they see with their dolls and stuffed animals. They rock, coo, sing, and play, all the while rehearsing for that great day when they have a child or children of their own. What do most little boys observe? They see Mom, a baby-sitter, or Granny doing the child care, nurturing the babies and comforting the toddlers. It is the rare male child who had a dad who actually participated actively in the child-rearing process, especially from the nurturing point of view. Dads have tended to be absent, busy, outside in the yard, at work, or on the phone. Many boys were not given much of a chance to develop good parenting skills before as men they actually became fathers.

Therefore, many men need their wives to model the correct behaviors and encourage them in their efforts. Did you know that many men fear handling a newborn baby and are afraid that they will inadvertently hurt the child? Such men need support to try out these new, risky parenting behaviors. They need nudging to risk and even take a few parenting classes, or read a book or two on being a great dad.

Affirm your man and his abilities to parent. If you see him succeeding, or doing something notable, say so. He may not express it, but he is worried that maybe he does not do an adequate job. You are the one who can reassure him if he does well and support his learning if he needs help.

And when you want to communicate with Mr. Right, do not just say, "Honey, we need to talk." That phrase scares men to death. To them, "talking" means interminable nagging or endless discussion. Men are problem solvers. Say something like, "Joe, we need to talk about Jenny's soccer practice. The conversation will take about ten minutes maximum. When is a good time?" That way your spouse will know the topic and time limit and be less apt to resist the conversation.

But by all means, communicate. *Never* expect that he already knows!

9. Be a Safe Harbor of Love

Nothing is more encouraging than to know you have a safe person in your life to go to when things are tough. When women are discouraged they want an empathetic ear. When they fail, they want an accepting hug. Men are just like women in this regard. They just do not ask so directly, or admit it as readily.

Life can be difficult. "Duh!" you say. Yet how many women do you know who like to complain about their husbands to other women? Granted, some men do the same when they get together with the guys, but your Mr. Right needs a woman who accepts him, warts and all. He wants a woman with whom he can fail, goof up, make a jerk of himself, and still be loved and accepted, not ridiculed.

What can make you a safe person for your man? Here are a few characteristics that you might consider cultivating:

Humility. Only someone who understands her own fallibility and weakness is going to be humble enough to accept her man's flaws. This concept does not mean that you are so humble you fail to maintain standards, boundaries, or accountability. It means you are enough aware of your own brokenness that you do not need to rejoice in his failures. It means having enough honesty about your own flaws that you can empathize with him when he struggles with the ones he has.

Ability to listen nonjudgmentally. Unconditional acceptance is not sentimentalism or being so open-minded you let your brains fall out. It means that you know how to keep your opinions to yourself in deference to the need of the moment. It means knowing how to listen constructively without making condescending nonverbal responses such as rolling your eyes or looking disgusted.

Safe people are great listeners. They encourage others to continue talking by using open-ended questions or statements such as "Tell me more about that" or "What made you come to that realization?" or "What do you mean when you say you feel . . . ?"

Confidentiality and trustworthiness. Your man will feel much more able to talk to you if he knows he can trust you. If he suspects that you share everything he says with your girlfriends or your mother, he will be reluctant to come to you with his struggles.

Aware of your limits. Safe people know what they can do and what they cannot do. They are not martyrs in their relationships with family, friends, or spouse. They have a realistic assessment of their gifts and capabilities, and do not try to inappropriately take over and fix someone else's problems.

10. KEEP YOUR SECURITY IN THE LORD

Mr. Right may be wonderful, but he does not want to be placed on a pedestal. Adoration belongs to God alone! We all want to be loved, desired, and cherished, but no one who is healthy wants to be the center of someone else's life. And no man, no matter how marvelous, can bear that burden. Being placed on such a high pedestal makes a man feel hypocritical because he knows that no one is that good. He will feel as if he can never meet your expectations if you revere him too much. Admiration, affection, respect—yes! Adoration, worship, elevation to sainthood—never!

11. SHARE YOUR STRUGGLES

Do not be afraid to reveal your own struggles and hurts, especially the ones you experience in your relationship with God. Sometimes women seem as if they have it all together, so their men hesitate to talk about their fears, doubts, and struggles. We all have good days and bad days. We have times when we are on a spiritual mountaintop and days when God does not seem to exist. If the only side of yourself that your Mr. Right sees is the superspiritual side, he could come to resent you. Who wants to hang around someone who is so perfect?

Mr. Rights wants to be strong for you too. He wants to be your knight in shining armor. (Really. A recent survey showed that both women and men still cling nostalgically to that notion of the guy being the rescuer or hero!)

Just as you want to know and feel that your husband needs you, so Mr. Right wants to know and feel that you need him. He wants to shelter you. This is not because you are a weak, wimpy female who cannot do anything for herself, but because you are the woman he loves. An unhealthy man wants a dependent woman. Mr. Right wants someone who can be interdependent, who knows how to receive and to give. How much fun would it be if you never were allowed to do any caretaking, loving, or nurturing because your man did not want to be so weak as to "need" you? Well, men like to be needed as well.

12. FORGIVE AND FORGET

One of the most endearing qualities in a spouse is her ability to forgive. Have you ever messed up so bad that you figured the relationship was doomed—and then you found out that your friend, parent, sibling, coach, or relative had the gracious ability to forgive you? What an exhilarating feeling to be free of the guilt, the shame, and the remorse; to rest again in that person's good graces; to not have your failure flung in your face every time you have a disagreement.

To feel forgiven at a deep level is an awesome thing. It is a gift you can give your Mr. Right. It is a gift he will treasure if he is wise, and not abuse if he is humble.

Holding a grudge is one of the most destructive things anyone can do to herself or to someone else. Sometimes we think that we are "getting back" at the person by holding the grudge, or that somehow we are more powerful when we hold a failure in someone's face. Yet the reality is that grudges make us sick physically, emotionally, and spiritually, and they further destroy a broken relationship. We need to forgive freely so that we and the other are no longer bound by the sin or mistake. Forgiveness is a step in restoring the relationship. There is more to restoration than forgiveness, but it is a first step.

Your Mr. Right is going to fail you, hurt you, and disappoint you somewhere, somehow. Just as you are going to fail, hurt, and disappoint him. When he does, the best gift you can give him is forgiving and forgetting, as God in Christ has forgiven you and forgotten your sins. Nothing encourages a relationship more than forgiving.

One of God's purposes in marriage is to use each spouse to help the other grow in every area of life. None of us is so together, so mature that we could not use some encouragement, challenge, or even rebuke from someone who loves us unconditionally. You have a chance to be a positive influence with your Mr. Right, to be an instrument of grace that helps him become even better. Take it.

A BRIEF REVIEW

In an effort to make the complex as simple as possible, we have pulled together summaries of the best way to find Mr. Right.

Mr. Right is looking for a woman who is:

- Approachable.
- Genuine. Mr. Right does not want you to feign a interest in football if you detest it.
- Accepting.
- Sexually healthy and interested.
- Spiritually and ethically committed.
- Moderate.
- Educated and able to support herself.
- Wise.
- Fun! Not that life is always a party, but a healthy relationship has a strong amount of joy and laughter.

- Active. Ms. Right is not a couch potato.

- Interested in a relationship.

- Loving. She wants to bring out the best in her man.

- Whole.

- Stable. No one wants a flake. A good man is looking for a partner who will be an asset to his life, not a liability.

- A companion. Men value doing things *with* a woman.

- Someone who laughs!

- A homemaker. Men look to women to create the home atmosphere.

- A communicator. Men hate playing "Read My Mind."

- An affirmer. Men long to be appreciated and respond generously to it.

- A lover.

Your role in finding Mr. Right is:

- Be Ms. Right.

- Make the most of your physical appearance without being obsessed with it.

- Know what you are looking for: don't take the first man who walks by. Have a standard by which to discern who is Mr. Right and who is Mr. Wrong.

- Take your time. Rome wasn't built in a day and neither are healthy relationships.

- Keep growing as a person. If you are boring, how will you attract someone interesting?

- Know your standard sexually, and stick to it. Be sure that standard is sex *after* marriage. Mr. Right is not looking for an easy woman.

- Keep your sense of humor. Nothing is more unattractive than a sourpuss.

- Look in the right places. You won't find Mr. Right by staring at the television set in your family room. Get out there and mingle.

- Let friends and family know you are interested in finding a life partner. Let friends fix you up.

- Be hospitable. Make your house the place people want to come visit.

- Be approachable, genuine, and honest.

Disguises worn by Mr. Wrong:

- Mr. Moneybags: just because a man is a millionaire does not make him Mr. Right.

- Mr. Supersuccess: business or financial success has nothing to do with success in a relationship. Be sure if he has one, he also has the other.

- Mr. Status Symbol: prestige is nice, but it is very superficial.

- Mr. Wonderful, alias Mr. Perfect: if he seems too good to be true, he probably is.

- Mr. Superstar: the chances of his being your Mr. Right are small. Most of these types are more in love with themselves than with anyone else.

- Mr. Stud, alias Mr. Romance: this guy will sweep you off your feet and get your hormones racing, but that is all he has in mind.

- Mr. Sensitive: many mama's boys appear to be quite sensitive; so do some who are having struggles with their own sexuality. Be sure sensitivity is balanced and healthy.
- Mr. Faithful: make sure his "faith" is genuine.
- Mr. Humble: he is really a coward.
- Mr. Empathy: in conversation, if you consistently reveal more than he does, watch out.

Mr. Right is Mr. Not Right Now if:

- He is newly divorced (less than two years) and/or not over his last relationship.
- He is unwilling to commit to you with a ring and a date.
- He is obsessed with other attractive women or is easily distracted by them.
- He still lives at home and seems overly attached to Mom and/or Dad.
- He has a pile of debt and no responsible plan to pay it off.
- He is angry at God for unanswered prayers, loss, death, or tragedy.
- He pushes you for more commitment than you are ready for.
- He is depressed and/or has *recently* been diagnosed with a serious mental or neurobiological disorder.

Disasters you can avoid include:

- Having sex on the first date or any date before the wedding.

- Expecting that you can make a silk purse out of a sow's ear. You cannot turn Mr. Wrong into Mr. Right, no matter how much you love him.

- Expecting to "hook up" with any number of sex partners *now*, and be able to easily shift gears and develop an intimate, healthy relationship with Mr. Right when he appears.

- Expecting to find Mr. Right in all the wrong places. You won't find a prince in a pigpen.

- Expecting Mr. Right to make up for what Daddy did not give you.

- Dating or getting too friendly with a married man.

- Getting involved with a man who abandoned his wife and children.

- Seducing a man into leaving his wife and family.

- Ignoring the fact that your background, beliefs, and values are totally different.

- Getting swept off your feet in a whirlwind romance. He may be Mr. Right, but love waits, lust doesn't.

Destroy Mr. Right by:

- Expecting him to be perfect. He may be right for you, but he is not, and never will be, perfect.

- Spoiling him by being a doormat, a wimp, a mouse. Giving Mr. Right everything his heart desires can turn him into Mr. Brat real quickly.

- Expecting him to be a carbon copy of your father.

- Comparing him at every opportunity to all the other men you dated or the men your friends married.

- Never disagreeing. Do not withhold genuine feedback because he might be hurt or angry.

- Nagging him when he fails to do what you want when you want it done.

- Smothering and worshiping him.

- Telling him what to do. Mr. Right does not marry to replace his mother.

- Never holding him accountable.

- Withholding sex when his is not exactly what you want him to be.

- When kids come along, forgetting he exists and focusing obsessively on them.

- Ceasing to grow and change and learn.

- Always expecting him to make more money than last year.

- Laughing at him when he is weak or vulnerable.

- Forgetting to pray for him every day.

Improve Mr. Right by:

- Encouraging, affirming, appreciating him. We all know the benefits of positive reinforcement.

- Accepting him as he is, acknowledging his strengths and his weaknesses.

- Understanding the enormous pressure a man feels to succeed.

- Understanding that he may not realize that what works with the guys may not work with you and the kids.

- Treating him with dignity (respect) and admiration, and expect it in return.

- Helping him to have more fun. Surprise him once in a while.

- Balancing his weaknesses with your strengths.

- Keeping yourself centered on your relationship with God—not on him.

- Teaching him how to be a better husband and father. If women do not communicate about what they or their children need, men can only guess.

- Sharing your own spiritual struggles and doubts.

- Remembering to forgive as Christ has forgiven you.

- providing a safe harbor for his love. Make sure he knows that in your arms he will find love, honesty, and grace.

Thank you for giving us your time with this book. If it has helped you, please share it with friend.

You can contact Steve Arterburn at Sarterburn@newlife.com, and Meg Rinck at meg3124@prodigy.net

NOTES

INTRODUCTION

1. "Flying Solo: Single by Choice," Time, 28 August 2000, 47–55.
2. Patrick McHenry, Ohio State University sociologist, cited by Marilyn Elias, *USA Today* article, run by *Cincinnati Enquirer*, Summer 2000.

CHAPTER 10

1. These personality types are adapted from I. B. Myers, The Myers-Briggs Personality Inventory (Palo Alto: Consulting Psychological Press, Inc., 1980).

CHAPTER 11

1. "The Web's Dark Side: Investigative Report," *US News and World Report*, 28 August 2000, pp. 36–45.
2. Ibid.
3. Ibid.
4. Ibid.
5. Ibid.

NOTES

CHAPTER 12

1. Raymond C. McGraine, *The Body Language of Flirting, Dating, and Romance* (1998), pp. 8–32.

2. Vera Lee, *How to Flirt: A Step by Step Guide to Bewitching a Man Outrageously* (Newton, MA: Olympia Press, 1998).

3. Vera Lee, *How to Flirt*, 44–45.

Discover if you are in love with Mr. Wrong by taking this quiz. If you want to know even more, read *Avoiding Mr. Wrong (And What To Do If You Didn't): Ten Men Who Will Ruin Your Life.*

ISBN 0-7852-6889-8

ARE YOU IN LOVE WITH MR. WRONG?

1. Does he flare up and lose his temper over small things and at times threatens or becomes violent? ❑ yes ❑ no

2. Does he become inordinately jealous or resent your relationships with others and frequently becomes picky, controlling, and rigid? ❑ yes ❑ no

3. Is he unable to break his allegiance with his mom and her feelings, desires, and demands, leaving you feeling like the "other woman" in the relationship? ❑ yes ❑ no

4. Are his stories and explanations hard to believe and you often feel in your gut that he is hiding something and deceiving you? ❑ yes ❑ no

5. Do you end up paying for most of the things you do together because he sponges off others, using you and them financially and otherwise to cover his irresponsibility? ❑ yes ❑ no

6. Is he so passive and preoccupied that communication with him is either impossible or like pulling teeth? ❑ yes ❑ no

7. Has your relationship with him taken a backseat to his obsessive and compulsive relationship with work, chemicals, alcohol, sex, gambling, pornography, sports, or even church? ❑ yes ❑ no

8. Is he indifferent to matters of faith, values, and morality; intimating that church and religion are for women and the weak? ❑ yes ❑ no

9. Does he seem "too good to be true" and able to charm anyone he meets? ❑ yes ❑ no

10. Is he afraid to take a stand or set boundaries with you or the kids and is such a people pleaser that he goes along with the crowd, even when he knows it is not right for you, him, or your relationship? ❑ yes ❑ no

Each question refers to a specific Mr. Wrong who will make your life miserable. So if you answered yes to any of the questions, you are most likely in love with a Mr. Wrong. If you checked more than one, he must be really wrong. Here is the key to discovering which Mr. Wrong is in your life:

(1) Mr. Angry, (2) Mr. Control Freak, (3) Mr. Mama's Boy, (4) Mr. Deceiver, (5) Mr. Eternal Kid, (6) Mr. Detachment, (7) Mr. Addiction, (8) Mr. Ungodly, (9) Mr. Wonderful, (10) Mr. Cowardly Lion

HAVE YOU EVER BEEN SO IN LOVE YOU COULDN'T THINK STRAIGHT? FORTUNATELY, YOU CAN STILL READ.

Find the help you need to clear your head in Stephen Arterburn's new book, *Avoiding Mr. Wrong.* Discover why you might be attracted to unsuitable, even destructive men— and they to you. More than a checklist of men to steer clear of, it's a powerful tool to help you see more clearly and act more wisely in pursuit of God's best for you—and his name is Mr. Right.

$18.99

Find out more about the men who are not worth the trouble they cause:

1. The Detached Man
2. The Control Freak
3. Mr. Wonderful
4. The Cowardly Lion
5. The Angry Man
6. The Mama's Boy
7. The Deceiver
8. The Addict
9. The Eternal Kid
10. The Ungodly Man

"If you combine your knowledge of men with a new awareness of yourself," write the authors, "you have gone a long way in avoiding Mr. Wrong." Only when you can consistently avoid Mr. Wrong will you be closer to finding Mr. Right.

THOMAS NELSON
Since 1798

For other products and live events, visit us at: **thomasnelson.com**

ABOUT THE AUTHORS

STEPHEN ARTERBURN is the founder and chairman of New Life Clinics, the largest provider of Christian counseling and treatment throughout the United States and Canada and is also the host of the daily *New Life Live*, national radio program heard on over one hundred outlets and at www.newlife.com. Arterburn is the creator of the Women of Faith conferences and the bestselling author of more than 30 books, including *Avoiding Mr. Wrong; More Jesus, Less Religion; The Seven Keys to Spiritual Renewal;* and *Mastering Your Moods.* Mr. Arterburn has appeared on numerous nationally televised talk shows and has been featured in publications such as the *New York Times, USA Today, Time* and *Reader's Digest.* He resides with his family in Laguna Beach, California.

MARGARET J. RINCK is a clinical psychologist, author, and ordained clergy and is a professional counselor with New Life Clinics. She is the author of *Christian Men Who Hate Women; Healing Hurting Relationships* (Zondervan 1990), and co-author of *Avoiding Mr. Wrong (And What to Do if You Didn't): Ten Men Who Will Ruin Your Life* (Thomas Nelson Publishers, 2000). Dr. Rinck lives in Cincinnati, Ohio.

OTHER BOOKS BY STEPHEN ARTERBURN

OTHER BOOKS BY MARGARET RINCK

Avoiding Mr. Wrong
Can Christians Love Too Much? Breaking the Cycle of Codependency,
Zondervan, 1989
Christian Men Who Hate Women: Healing Hurting Relationships,
Zondervan, 1989
"Christian Men Who Hate Women" in *Healing the Hurting: Giving Hope
and Help to the Abused Woman,* ed. by Kroeger and Beck,
Baker Books, 1998
Finding Mr. Right,
Thomas Nelson, 2001